Future Leadership: Navigating the Challenges of the 21st Century

From Global Cultures and Digital Innovation to Mental Health and Strategic Vision: A Comprehensive Guide for Modern Leaders

David Winston

1. **Definition of Leadership**: Exploring the difference between "management" and "leadership."

2. **History of Leadership**: How theories of leadership have evolved over time.

3. **Characteristics of Effective Leaders**: Inherent and acquired qualities that distinguish successful leaders.

4. **Traditional Leadership Theories**: For example, trait theories, behavioral theories, and situational theories.

5. **Contemporary Leadership Theories**: Transformational leadership, servant leadership, authentic leadership, and other emerging models.

6. **Leadership and Power**: Types of power and how they are wielded by leaders.

7. **Culture and Leadership**: How different cultures influence leadership styles and expectations.

8. **Female Leadership**: The importance and uniqueness of female leadership in the modern context.

9. **Challenges of Leadership**: Conflict management, active listening, empathy, and resilience.

10. **Leadership and Ethics**: The moral responsibility of leaders and the importance of integrity.

11. **Techniques and Tools**: Tools and techniques for enhancing leadership skills.

12. **Leadership and Innovation**: How leaders can promote and support innovation.

13. **Leadership Training**: The significance of ongoing training and leadership development.

14. **Case Studies**: Real examples of leadership in action, successes, and failures.

15.   **Digital Leadership**: The importance of leadership in the digital age and navigating digital transformation.

16.   **Leadership and Mental Health**: Stress management, burnout prevention, and self-care for leaders.

17.   **Teams and Leadership**: Creating, leading, and maintaining high-performance teams.

18.   **Vision and Mission**: The importance of having a clear vision and mission to guide actions and decisions.

19.   **Feedback and Leadership**: The importance of continuous feedback for growth and adaptation.

20.   **Future Trends**: Where is leadership headed? Exploring future perspectives.

1. Definition of Leadership and Its Distinction from Management

Definition of Leadership Leadership is often defined as the art of motivating a group of people to act towards a common goal. It is the ability to influence and guide others, to establish a vision, and to provide people with the motivation, guidance, and resources to achieve that vision.

Leadership vs. Management While "leadership" and "management" are often used interchangeably, they represent distinct and complementary concepts:

- **Management:** Focuses primarily on organization, planning, problem-solving, and achieving predefined goals. A manager is often concerned with ensuring that day-to-day operations run smoothly. This may include resource planning, budget management, team or project organization, and ensuring efficient resource utilization.
- **Leadership:** Involves inspiration, motivation, and the creation of a vision or direction for an organization or group of people. Leaders often work to establish a culture, develop people's potential, and navigate through changes. While a manager might be focused on "how" to do things, a leader is often focused on the "why."

Common Characteristics Although there are key differences between leadership and management, there are some overlapping qualities:

- **Effective Communication:** Both leaders and managers must be able to communicate clearly and effectively with their teams.
- **Decision-Making:** The ability to make decisions, sometimes in high-pressure situations or with limited information, is essential for both managers and leaders.
- **Accountability:** Both are responsible for their teams or departments and the decisions they make.

Distinction between Leadership and Management Leadership sits at the intersection of the ability to direct and the ability to inspire. While direction may involve organizing people and resources toward a specific goal, leadership goes beyond this. It's a combination of vision, charisma, integrity, and empathy that not only encourages others to follow but also believe in the path you've set.

One of the most distinctive aspects of leadership is influence. A leader influences through their behavior, words, and actions. It's not so much what a leader says, but how they say it and, most importantly, how they act. This consistency between words and actions often sets true leaders apart from those who simply hold positions of power.

On the other hand, management, while essential in every organization or team, tends to have a narrower focus. Management is concerned with efficiency, order, processes, and procedures. The manager ensures resources are allocated correctly, processes are followed, and goals are met in a timely manner.

One of the key distinctions between leadership and management lies in vision versus execution. While a leader looks to the future, envisioning what could be and outlining a clear path to achieve that possibility, a manager is often anchored in the present, focused on "how" rather than "what" or "why."

It's important to emphasize that neither leadership nor management is superior to the other; they are complementary. An organization needs visionaries who can point the way and inspire others to follow. At the same time, it needs competent individuals who can organize resources, plan execution, and ensure the vision becomes a reality.

One common mistake in organizations is assuming that a good manager is automatically a good leader and vice versa. This is not always the case. Some individuals are naturally gifted for leadership but may struggle with the nuances of management. Similarly, an exceptional manager who knows how to make an operation efficient may not have the skills or desire to inspire and lead others.

Leadership skills can be cultivated and developed, just as management skills can. Training, experience, and reflection are all essential components of growth as both a leader and a manager.

The context in which an individual operates can also influence the need for leadership versus management. For example, in crisis situations, strong leadership may be required to navigate uncertainty and establish a clear direction. On the other hand, in situations where processes and procedures need to be stabilized or improved, management skills may be more valuable.

Additionally, organizational culture plays a fundamental role in determining the balance between leadership and management. Some cultures value innovation, creativity, and long-term vision, all areas where leadership is essential. Other cultures may place a higher value on efficiency, precision, and compliance, areas where management skills are particularly valuable.

Finally, it's crucial to recognize that while leadership and management have distinct roles, there is also overlap. An effective leader must have some understanding of management to ensure their vision can be realized. Similarly, an effective manager can benefit from understanding elements of leadership to inspire and motivate their team toward operational excellence.

Leadership and Management: Two Sides of the Same Coin

Leadership, while often intertwined with **management**, is like two sides of the same coin. To understand the depth of their relationship and their distinction, it is helpful to further explore the nature and nuances of each.

Leadership at its core is about vision. A leader looks beyond the horizon, perceiving possibilities and potential changes before they manifest. Leadership is synonymous with anticipation: forecasting trends, recognizing emerging opportunities, and, equally important, identifying challenges before they become critical. This ability to anticipate is fueled by intuition but also by deep listening, understanding people, and available data.

Management, on the other hand, is concerned with the "here and now." While a leader might look to the stars, a manager focuses on solid ground, ensuring that day-to-day operations are conducted smoothly. But this does not mean that management is less important than leadership. Without effective management, the visions and aspirations of the leader would remain mere ideas. Management is what translates vision into tangible reality.

Another distinctive aspect of leadership is the ability to take calculated risks. Leaders, by their nature, are predisposed to challenge the status quo, seeking to break conventional barriers and push people and organizations outside their comfort zones. This disposition toward risk, however, is not reckless. It is informed by data, research, and, above all, active listening to people both inside and outside the organization.

In contrast, management tends to be more conservative. The manager's role is to minimize risks and ensure that operations are conducted predictably and consistently. This requires keen attention to detail, a deep understanding of processes, and strong organizational skills.

Another distinction relates to the nature of relationships. Leadership, at its best, is relational. Leaders create deep bonds with those around them, based on trust, empathy, and mutual respect. They recognize that true power does not come from position or authority but from the ability to connect, influence, and inspire others.

Managers, while also having important relationships, tend to have more functional relationships. These relationships are often shaped by roles, tasks, and responsibilities. For a manager, people are essential to achieving specific goals and metrics.

It is essential to recognize that, despite these distinctions, leadership and management are not mutually exclusive. A leader can exhibit managerial qualities, and a manager can prove to be an inspirational leader. The key lies in balancing these roles and recognizing when it's time to dream and when it's time to execute.

In Summary, leadership and management represent two fundamental and complementary aspects of leading groups, teams, or organizations. While leadership is oriented toward vision, innovation, and inspiration, management emphasizes efficiency, order, and implementation.

Leadership is inherently tied to the ability to see beyond the present, envisioning a desirable future, and mobilizing individuals toward that vision. Leaders have the profound responsibility of creating a sense of purpose and direction. This role requires empathy, active listening, and the ability to make decisions that can, at times, be unpopular or difficult. Leadership is about building bonds based on trust, empowering people, and creating an environment where individuals feel valued and understood.

On the other hand, management is the art of ensuring that an entity's day-to-day operations are conducted efficiently and consistently. Management requires meticulous attention to detail, a thorough understanding of processes, and the ability to coordinate resources and people to achieve specific objectives. A manager must be able to set priorities, allocate resources efficiently, and monitor progress to ensure goals are met.

However, the distinction between leadership and management is not rigid. In fact, in successful organizations, these two functions often intersect and integrate. An effective leader must have a solid understanding of management principles, while a successful manager will greatly benefit from incorporating leadership qualities into their approach.

The balance between leadership and management is crucial. Too much leadership without management can lead to grand visions without implementation, while excessive management without leadership can result in a stagnant, directionless organization. Success lies in the ability to balance and integrate these two aspects, ensuring that an inspiring vision is supported by solid and effective management. Ultimately, both leadership and management are essential for the prosperity and longevity of any organization or initiative.

2. History of Leadership: How Leadership Theories Have Evolved Over Time

The evolution of leadership theories can be traced through centuries of human history, but here, we will primarily focus on developments in the 20th and 21st centuries. During this period, the understanding of leadership underwent a series of conceptual revolutions, moving from trait-based approaches to theories based on behavior, contingency, and transformation, to name a few.

1. **Trait-Based Theories (Early 20th Century):** These theories focused on attempting to identify inherent traits or physical and psychological characteristics that make a person a leader. It was believed that leaders were born, not made. Studies sought to identify common traits such as intelligence, determination, self-confidence, and courage.

2. Behavioral Theories (1950s and 1960s): These theories moved away from the notion that leaders were "born" and instead focused on the specific actions of leaders. The idea was that by studying the behaviors of effective leaders, leadership could be taught through training and development. Major studies in this field were conducted by universities such as Ohio State and the University of Michigan.

3. Situational or Contingency Theories (1960s and 1970s): These theories recognized that there is no single effective leadership style for every situation. Instead, a leader's effectiveness depends on their ability to adapt to the context. Fiedler, Hersey, and Blanchard are among the key theorists in this domain.

4. Participative Leadership Theories (1970s): These theories suggest that the best leadership emerges from collaboration between leaders and followers. Some approaches, like Hersey and Blanchard's Situational Leadership Theory, emphasized the importance of follower maturity and capability in determining the appropriate leadership style.

5. Transformational and Transactional Theories (1980s and 1990s): While transactional theories view leadership as an exchange between leaders and followers (e.g., rewards for performance), transformational theories see leaders as charismatic figures who inspire and motivate their followers through vision, passion, and charisma. James MacGregor Burns and Bernard Bass are key figures in this field.

6. Competency-Based and Authentic Approaches (2000s): Competency-based leadership focuses on the skills and abilities that leaders must possess and develop. Authentic leadership emphasizes the leader's authenticity, consistency between values, thoughts, and actions.

7. Holistic and Spiritual Theories (2010s): These theories view leadership not only as a set of skills or behaviors but as an inner journey, tied to personal growth, awareness, and spirituality.

8. Contemporary Developments: With the advent of the digital age, social media, and globalization, leadership is still evolving. 21st-century leadership requires an understanding of global challenges, cultural diversity, technology, and rapid changes.

Through these evolutions, one thing remains constant: leadership is fundamental to guiding groups and organizations to success. Understanding how leadership theory has developed over time provides valuable insight into how the concept of leadership will continue to evolve in the future.

Certainly! Continuing on the history of leadership, we can see that, in addition to the main theories listed, there have been many other schools of thought and influences that have contributed to shaping our understanding of leadership over the centuries.

The Origins of Leadership: Tracing the Evolution of Leadership Theories

The origins of leadership can be traced back to ancient times when charismatic figures like kings, priests, and tribal leaders held power. In many ancient societies, leadership was often determined by birthright, physical strength, or oratorical abilities. For example, in ancient Greece, rhetoric was highly regarded, and those who could speak well and persuade others often rose to positions of power.

With the advent of major world religions such as Christianity, Islam, and Buddhism, new conceptions of leadership emerged. These religions introduced ideas of service, sacrifice, and moral guidance. Figures like Jesus Christ, Muhammad, and Buddha were not only seen as religious leaders but also as examples of leadership in terms of character, compassion, and vision.

During the Renaissance, with the awakening of critical thinking and humanism, a new idea of leadership emerged, one that recognized the importance of the individual and their unique abilities. Great thinkers like Machiavelli began to reflect on power, authority, and the nature of leadership, proposing that the end justifies the means.

The Industrial Revolution of the 18th and 19th centuries brought further changes. With the growth of factories and businesses, the need for effective management and organizational leaders became increasingly evident. Leadership was no longer just a matter of birthright or personal charisma but also required organizational skills and decision-making abilities.

The world wars of the 20th century and subsequent geopolitical tensions further evolved the understanding of leadership. Leaders like Winston Churchill, Franklin D. Roosevelt, and Martin Luther King Jr. emerged not only for their strategic and decision-making abilities but also for their capacity to inspire and unite people in challenging times.

In more recent times, with the rise of globalization, leadership has become even more complex. Today's leaders must navigate multicultural contexts, taking into account diverse norms, values, and expectations. They must also address unprecedented challenges such as climate change, economic inequalities, and political tensions.

With the advent of technology and social media, leadership has also become more transparent. Today's leaders are under scrutiny like never before. This has led to a greater emphasis on ethics, integrity, and accountability.

Another noteworthy aspect is the rise of female leadership. For centuries, leadership has been dominated by men due to patriarchal structures. However, in the 20th and 21st centuries, more and more women have begun to assume leadership positions in various fields, challenging traditional norms and offering new perspectives and approaches.

Finally, the growing understanding of psychology and neuroscience has begun to influence leadership theories. With a deeper understanding of how people's minds work, leadership theorists can now explore more deeply what motivates, inspires, and influences human behavior in leadership contexts. This has led to a greater emphasis on emotional intelligence, self-awareness, and psychological well-being as key components of effective leadership.

At the core of contemporary conceptions of leadership is the idea that a leader is not simply someone who holds a high office or title; rather, leadership is seen as a relational process through which a person influences others to achieve a common goal.

With increasing globalization, the definition of leadership has been influenced by diverse cultures and traditions. For example, while the Western approach to leadership may emphasize autonomy, decision-making, and individualism, other cultures may place greater emphasis on collaboration, harmony, and consensus. In Asia, for instance, Confucian philosophy places great emphasis on respect, harmony, and balance in all relationships, and this also influences local conceptions of leadership.

Contemporary Leadership Trends: Navigating a Complex Landscape

Organizations are moving away from rigid hierarchical structures towards more flexible and networked models. This has led to the emergence of what is often referred to as "distributed leadership" or "shared leadership," where leadership is no longer the exclusive domain of a single individual or a small group but rather a collective process.

The advent of the digital age has introduced new challenges and opportunities for leaders. The explosion of social media platforms has changed the dynamics of communication. Now, a tweet or a Facebook post can have an immediate impact on the public perception of a leader or an organization. This hyper-connectivity has made reputation and personal brand management even more crucial for today's leaders.

In the context of technological innovation, new forms of leadership are also emerging. Leadership in the era of artificial intelligence, for example, requires a deep understanding not only of people but also of machines and systems. This means that leaders must keep pace with rapid technological advancements while also maintaining a strong ethical foundation given the power and capabilities of emerging technologies.

An interesting trend in recent years is the increasing focus on resilience in leadership. In a rapidly changing world, leaders must be able to cope with failures, setbacks, and crises while remaining centered and focused. This has led to a greater emphasis on the development of personal and organizational resilience as a key leadership competency.

At the same time, there has been a growing awareness of the importance of the mental and physical well-being of leaders. Leadership can be extremely demanding and stressful, and the ability to take care of oneself, manage stress, and maintain a work-life balance has become fundamental.

Another noteworthy development is the growing importance of "sustainable leadership." This concept involves a leader's ability to lead in a way that is sustainable not only for the organization but also for society and the environment. This trend reflects an increasing awareness of environmental and social issues and the responsibility of leaders to proactively address them.

Overall, while the foundations of leadership may remain constant, the form and function of leadership are continually evolving. Today's leaders must navigate a complex, uncertain, and interconnected landscape, requiring a combination of adaptive skills, knowledge, and mindsets.

The history of leadership is deeply intertwined with the evolution of human society and changes in political, economic, social, and technological contexts. Each era has had its distinct models and theories of leadership, reflecting the challenges and needs of its time.

From ancient tribal societies where leadership was based on strength and protection, through historical epochs in which religion, philosophy, and politics redefined what it meant to be a leader, to the industrial and technological revolutions that revolutionized organizational structures and how people interact and communicate, leadership has continued to evolve.

The essence of leadership is not only found in personal abilities or technical skills but rather in an individual's capacity to influence, inspire, and mobilize people toward the achievement of a shared vision or goal. This core remains constant, despite changes in how leadership is exercised or perceived.

In recent times, the complexity of global issues - ranging from climate change to economic inequalities, from digital transformation to geopolitical conflicts - requires a new generation of leaders who are versatile, ethically guided, and capable of operating in diverse and interconnected contexts. These leaders, in addition to having a solid understanding of local contexts, must also be globally savvy, able to connect the dots between seemingly disparate issues and see the big picture.

Twenty-first-century leadership also places unprecedented emphasis on the importance of diversity and inclusion. As organizations and societies become increasingly diverse, the ability to understand, appreciate, and harness this diversity becomes crucial. This means that leaders must now be sensitive to cultural, gender, age, and other forms of diversity and use this understanding to create environments where everyone feels valued and can perform at their best.

In conclusion, the history of leadership is not just a narrative of how theories and practices have evolved over time, but it is also a testament to the human desire for progress, innovation, and a sense of purpose. As we face the challenges of the future, it is essential to reflect on the lessons of the past and integrate them with new ideas and approaches, ensuring that leadership continues to evolve in ways that are relevant, effective, and in service of the common good.

3. Characteristics of Effective Leaders: Innate and Acquired Qualities that Distinguish Successful Leaders

The characteristics of effective leaders have been the focus of studies and discussions for centuries. While some people believe that leaders are "born," there is a growing awareness of the importance of learning and development in shaping a successful leader. The characteristics of effective leaders can be divided into innate and acquired qualities, although these two categories often overlap and influence each other. Here's an analysis of these characteristics:

Innate Qualities:

1. **Intuition:** Some leaders have an incredible ability to "sense" the right direction or anticipate problems and opportunities before they become evident.
2. **Charisma:** This magnetic quality can inspire others to follow and rally behind a vision or goal.
3. **Self-awareness:** While it can be developed over time, a natural inclination toward self-reflection can be seen as innate.
4. **Resilience:** The ability to stand tall and remain centered in the face of adversity is often rooted in an individual's personality.
5. **Passion:** A genuine passion for a cause or goal can be innate and drives leaders to pursue grand visions.

Acquired Qualities:

1. **Technical Competence:** This is knowledge and skill in a particular field or industry. An effective leader is well-versed in their sector.
2. **Communication Skills:** The ability to communicate clearly, persuasively, and effectively can be developed through education and practice.
3. **Strategic Thinking:** While some may have a natural inclination for this, strategic thinking can also be honed through education, training, and experience.
4. **Conflict Management:** An effective leader knows how to handle and resolve conflicts constructively.
5. **Continuous Learning:** Successful leaders recognize the importance of continuous learning and are committed to personal and professional development.
6. **Ethics and Integrity:** While some people may have a strong innate moral compass, the importance of acting with integrity can also be learned and internalized over time.
7. **Situational Leadership:** The ability to adapt one's leadership style to the specific needs of a situation or individual.
8. **Decision-Making Skills:** Making informed, timely, and sometimes tough decisions is a fundamental skill that can be developed.

A crucial point to emphasize is that while some people may have a natural predisposition for some of these characteristics, training, experience, mentorship, and continuous learning play a fundamental role in developing an effective leader. Additionally, the combination of these qualities and how they are applied can vary depending on the cultural, organizational, and situational context.

Leadership is not a static concept but rather a fluid and dynamic one, influenced by multiple internal and external factors. As we delve deeper into the characteristics of effective leaders, it becomes evident that these qualities are often interconnected, and their impact can be amplified when combined in unique ways.

Vision, for example, is not just about the ability to see where an organization or group could go in the future. It also involves the ability to communicate that vision in a way that people can see it, feel it, and, most importantly, feel a part of it. A leader who has a vision but cannot effectively communicate it may find it challenging to inspire others to follow.

Empathy is another crucial characteristic in contemporary leadership. It is the ability to put oneself in the shoes of others, to understand their experiences, emotions, and motivations. In a globalized and interconnected world, where leaders often interact with a wide range of stakeholders from diverse cultures and backgrounds, empathy becomes even more critical. For a leader, being empathetic can help build deeper relationships, prevent conflicts, and make more informed decisions that consider the needs and expectations of all stakeholders.

Another fundamental aspect of leadership is **flexibility**. In a rapidly changing work environment, leaders must be able to adapt quickly to new situations, learn from challenges, and remain open to new ideas and approaches. Rigidity can lead to missed opportunities and failure to recognize emerging threats. A flexible leader, on the other hand, will be able to navigate uncertainty, drive change, and help others adapt.

The importance of **organizational culture** cannot be underestimated. Effective leaders understand that they are not only guiding individuals but also shaping and influencing the culture of an entire organization. This involves establishing clear values, promoting positive behaviors, and ensuring mechanisms are in place to recognize and address negative behaviors. Culture, as it is often said, "eats strategy for breakfast." Therefore, a leader who disregards the current or desired culture of their organization may find that their strategies and visions fall short.

Modern Leadership Concepts and Skills: Adapting to a Changing Landscape

Collaboration is another key element. The days of the "command and control" leader are long gone. Today, leaders must be facilitators and coalition builders. They need to know how to work across functional, organizational, and geographical boundaries, bringing together people with diverse skills and perspectives to solve complex problems.

Lastly, there's the concept of **authenticity**. Authentic leaders are those who are true to themselves and others. They exhibit consistency between what they say and what they do, and they are not afraid to show vulnerability. This authenticity can help build trust, one of the fundamental pillars of any leadership relationship.

In a deeper analysis of the characteristics of effective leaders, it's essential to consider the vastness and complexity of the challenges leaders face today and how these challenges influence the required skills and qualities.

The holistic approach to leadership is an emerging trend. This approach considers the overall well-being of the leader: physical, mental, emotional, and spiritual. It's not just about leading others but also about self-care. A leader who is balanced in all these areas will be better equipped to handle stress, make decisions, and inspire others.

The concept of **distributed leadership** is another aspect to consider. This model argues that leadership should not be centralized in one person or a small group but rather distributed among many members of an organization. This encourages shared responsibilities and values the skills and knowledge of each individual. This type of leadership can be particularly effective in large organizations or situations where speed and agility are crucial.

Then there's the issue of **sustainability**. 21st-century leaders must look beyond short-term profit and consider the long-term impact of their decisions. This means thinking about environmental, social, and economic sustainability. Leaders who adopt a sustainable approach not only help protect the planet but also build goodwill and a positive reputation for their organizations.

Another key concept in modern leadership is **transparency**. In an era of immediate access to information and growing skepticism toward institutions, leaders must be open and transparent in their communications and decisions. This helps build trust and create a sense of belonging and inclusion among organization members.

A growth mindset, introduced by psychologist Carol Dweck, is another fundamental characteristic of effective leaders. This concept suggests that people can develop their abilities and skills through dedication and effort. Leaders with a growth mindset are open to feedback, see challenges as learning opportunities, and are constantly looking for ways to improve.

Cultural intelligence, in an increasingly globalized world, is essential. Leaders must be able to navigate and operate effectively in diverse cultures, understand cultural nuances and differences, and build bridges between people from different backgrounds.

Lastly, there's the ability to **anticipate and innovate**. Leaders of the future must always stay one step ahead, predicting emerging trends and adapting their organizations accordingly. Innovation is not just about new products or technologies but also new business models, new approaches to people management, and new strategies to address global challenges.

This ever-evolving landscape of leadership underscores the need for leaders to be adaptable, continuously learn, and remain open to new ideas and approaches.

In essence, leadership is as much an art as it is a science. The characteristics of effective leaders, while numerous and sometimes intangible, form a mosaic of qualities that can lead an individual to inspire, guide, and positively influence others.

First and foremost, a leader's **vision** is not merely a futuristic prediction but a well-defined ideal that translates into concrete goals and tangible strategies. Without a clear vision, leadership becomes a navigation exercise without a compass. However, having a vision is not enough: an effective leader must also possess the ability to convey this vision, making it palpable and understandable for everyone.

Empathy and **transparency**, beyond mere words, are essential human qualities for building a relationship of trust. In an era dominated by technology and information, people seek authenticity and sincerity. A leader who exhibits empathy and transparency can connect on a deeper level with their followers, earning their trust and respect.

Key Leadership Qualities in a Changing World

Flexibility and a **growth mindset** are essential in a rapidly evolving world. Leaders who adapt, learn, and grow from changes and challenges are the ones who steer organizations toward long-term success. They are the ones who not only accept change but embrace it as an inexhaustible source of opportunities.

The **holistic approach**, **sustainability**, and **cultural intelligence** reflect a leader who looks to the future. These characteristics indicate a deep understanding of the globalized world in which we operate and the myriad challenges it presents. They signify the wisdom to see beyond the immediate horizon and recognize the interconnections that exist in a global ecosystem.

Distributed leadership and **innovation** represent a departure from traditional models. Instead of centralizing power and decisions, distributed leadership recognizes the value of spreading responsibility and autonomy, fostering collaboration and ingenuity. Innovation, on the other hand, is the engine that drives forward, ensuring that a leader remains relevant and proactive in an ever-changing environment.

In summary, while the characteristics of an effective leader may vary depending on the context and culture, there are some universal traits that define great leadership. These traits, combined with the right skills and experience, can lead to transcendent leadership that not only achieves goals but also inspires and uplifts those who are led. In a world full of challenges and opportunities, effective leadership is more than ever a combination of vision, empathy, adaptability, and the relentless pursuit of excellence.

4. Traditional Leadership Theories: Examples include Trait, Behavioral, and Situational Theories

Traditional Leadership Theories: Traditional leadership theories have shaped our understanding of the essence and dynamics of leadership for many decades. Here's an analysis of the main traditional theories:

1. **Trait Theories:**

    - **Foundation:** These theories argue that specific traits or personal characteristics make a person predisposed to be an effective leader. These theories often stem from the belief that "leaders are born, not made."

- **Common Traits:** Some of the traits that often emerge in these theories include intelligence, determination, self-assurance, and integrity.

- **Limitations:** While some research has shown a correlation between certain traits and effective leadership, these theories have been criticized for not considering the importance of context or acquired skills.

2. **Behavioral Theories:**

   - **Foundation:** Unlike trait theories, behavioral theories contend that leadership is defined by what leaders do rather than who they are. These theories focus on the actions and behaviors of leaders rather than their personal traits or characteristics.

   - **Common Approaches:** Two of the most well-known behavioral models are the task-oriented approach (emphasizing goals and outcomes) and the relationship-oriented approach (emphasizing relationship-building and team well-being).

- **Limitations:** While behavioral theories provide a more dynamic snapshot of leadership compared to trait theories, they may not account for the specific nuances of situations or contexts in which leadership manifests.

3. **Situational (or Contingency) Theories:**

- **Foundation:** These theories suggest that leadership effectiveness depends on the combination of leadership styles and the specific situation. In other words, what works in one situation may not work in another.

- **Key Principles:** One of the most well-known models in this field is the Hersey-Blanchard Situational Leadership Model, which suggests that the leader should adapt their style (directive, persuasive, participative, or delegating) based on the "maturity" or competence and involvement of the follower.

- **Limitations:** While these theories offer a flexible framework, they can be complex to apply in practice as they require ongoing assessment and adaptation to changing circumstances.

4. Traditional leadership theories, while providing a fundamental starting point for the study of leadership, can be further explored through various lenses and dimensions.

5. Considering trait theories, it's interesting to note how, in antiquity, leadership was often seen in terms of physical characteristics. For example, in many ancient cultures, tall stature and a commanding physical presence were considered signs of a potential leader. This perspective has evolved over time. Contemporary research has focused on less tangible traits such as emotional intelligence, active listening skills, and open-mindedness. However, a constant challenge in trait theories is determining the ideal combination of traits and whether these traits can be developed or are innate.

6. Behavioral theories, on the other hand, have undergone significant evolution over the course of the 20th century. Initially, research focused on how leaders made decisions or assigned tasks. However, with the advent of more complex organizations and the growing importance of soft skills, attention shifted toward behaviors such as motivating, creating a positive work

environment, or managing conflicts. The increasing diversity in modern workplaces has also highlighted the need for leaders to demonstrate inclusivity, cultural sensitivity, and a fair work ethic.

7. Situational theories, above all, might be the most complex in terms of practical application. While the idea of adapting leadership style based on the situation is intuitively logical, reality presents a wide range of variables that can influence a situation. For example, how should a leader behave during a corporate crisis compared to a period of stability? And how should their techniques change if they are leading a startup versus an established multinational corporation? Or, how should a leader adapt when transitioning between different industries, each with its own culture and unique challenges?

8. Another noteworthy aspect is the growing influence of non-Western cultures on leadership theories. For example, concepts like "Wa" in Japan, emphasizing group harmony, or "Ubuntu" in Africa, focusing on human interconnectedness, offer alternative perspectives and further enrich our understanding of leadership.

9. Leadership is not limited to organizations or businesses. Think of leaders in social

movements, music, sports, or the arts. Each domain has its unique dynamics, and traditional leadership theories may not always directly apply. However, they provide a framework that can be adapted and modified, offering valuable insights into how people can lead in various contexts and situations.

Traditional Leadership Theories: For example, Trait, Behavioral, and Situational Theories

The Vast and Complex Landscape of Traditional Leadership Theories: The breadth and depth of traditional leadership theories reflect the complexity of the leadership concept itself. The ongoing research and analysis of these models provide us with new lenses through which we can observe and understand leadership in various contexts.

Key Considerations in Trait Theories: A key consideration in trait theories is the tension between nature and nurture. While it's true that certain traits may predispose an individual to leadership roles, upbringing and experience can play a crucial role in refining and developing these characteristics. For instance, while some individuals may have a natural predisposition for confidence or assertiveness, these qualities can also be developed through targeted exercises and constructive feedback. This raises intriguing questions about leader development and the potential for each individual to cultivate leadership skills.

The Primacy of Context in Behavioral Theories: In behavioral theories, the importance of context becomes paramount. For instance, leadership in a military context might require a more direct and hierarchical approach, while in a creative organization, a collaborative and democratic approach may be favored. Organizational culture also plays a significant role. Companies with an innovation-oriented culture may seek leaders who encourage experimentation and risk-taking, while those in more regulated industries may value predictability and consistency.

Dynamic Leadership in Situational Theories: Situational theories, in turn, remind us that leadership is not static. Leaders must be flexible and ready to adapt to changing circumstances. The ability to "read the room" and understand what is required in a given moment is crucial. For example, during a crisis, more frequent and direct communication may be necessary. However, once the crisis has passed, a "hands-off" approach and giving teams more autonomy may be more appropriate.

Ethical Intersection with Leadership: Another relevant aspect to consider is the intersection between leadership and ethics. Traditional theories have mainly focused on leadership effectiveness in terms of outcomes. However, there is a growing awareness of the importance of ethics in leadership. Being an effective leader doesn't just mean achieving goals but also acting with integrity, honesty, and respect for others.

Intercultural Understanding in a Global Context: Moreover, with globalization and the increasing interconnectedness of the world, intercultural understanding has become crucial for leadership. Western leadership theories may not always be directly applicable in non-Western contexts. Understanding and respecting cultural norms, values, and expectations are essential for effective leadership in a global context.

Leadership as a System: Finally, it's worth emphasizing that leadership is not just about individuals. While traditional theories tend to focus on the individual leader, group dynamics, organizational structures, and external influences also play a significant role in determining leadership effectiveness. This reminds us that leadership is an interconnected system, not merely a set of isolated traits or behaviors.

Comprehensive Insights from Traditional Leadership Theories: By comprehensively examining traditional leadership theories, we can draw some fundamental conclusions that outline the essence and complexity of leadership as a whole.

1. **Nature vs. Nurture in Trait Theories:** While there is consensus that certain traits may predispose an individual to leadership roles, it's also evident that the environment, education, and personal experiences play a crucial role in

shaping a leader. This underscores the importance of continuous training and learning on a leader's journey. Leaders are not born; they become leaders through a combination of innate predispositions and accumulated experiences.

2. **Flexibility in Behavioral Theories:** While certain behaviors may be effective in specific situations, a leader's ability to adapt and modify their style based on circumstances is fundamental. This requires a high degree of self-awareness, context understanding, and empathy toward others.

3. Adaptability of Situational Theories:

Leadership cannot be reduced to a formula or a rigid set of behaviors. Leaders must be prepared to navigate a constantly evolving landscape, requiring the ability to quickly assess situations and respond accordingly.

4. Ethics in Leadership: Beyond effectiveness, integrity and ethics are emerging as fundamental pillars of leadership. A leader cannot be effective in the long term without operating with strong moral principles. Trust, once lost, is challenging to regain.

5. Cultural Interconnectedness: Understanding the diverse cultural facets is indispensable in a globalized world. Today's and tomorrow's leaders must be able to cross cultural boundaries and integrate diverse perspectives while maintaining a core of universal principles and values.

6. Beyond the Individual: Although leadership is often viewed through the lens of the individual, it's essential to recognize that leadership also manifests through group dynamics, organizational cultures, and systemic interactions. Leadership is not just the act of leading but also the art of building, sustaining, and evolving an ecosystem in which people can thrive and achieve common goals.

In summary, while traditional leadership theories provide essential frameworks, it is crucial to view leadership as a dynamic and multifaceted concept. There is no one "one-size-fits-all" model for leadership; rather, the true art of leadership lies in an individual's ability to integrate knowledge, skills, values, and insights from various theories and apply them effectively in the various contexts they encounter.

5. Contemporary Leadership Theories: Transformational, Servant, Authentic Leadership, and other Emerging Models

Contemporary Leadership Theories: Research and the study of leadership have not stopped with traditional theories. Over time, as societies and organizations evolve, new theories have emerged to explain and guide leadership practices. Some of the most influential contemporary theories include:

1. **Transformational Leadership:** This theory focuses on the leader as a source of inspiration and motivation. Transformational leaders are those who stimulate and inspire their followers to achieve performance beyond expectations and

surpass their personal limits. These leaders tend to have a clear vision, show empathy, and consider the individual needs of their collaborators. Charismatic, inspiring, and with a clear vision, this form of leadership can lead to significant and lasting changes within an organization.

2. **Servant Leadership:** This model is based on the idea that a leader should primarily serve their employees, placing their needs at the center. These leaders focus on empowering and developing their teams rather than exerting power or authority. They believe in the potential of each individual and seek to create an environment where everyone can thrive and succeed.

3. **Authentic Leadership:** This theory emphasizes the importance of authenticity in leadership. Authentic leaders are self-aware, have a deep understanding of themselves, and are guided by personal values and principles. This type of leadership promotes transparency, honesty, and consistency.

4. **Participative Leadership:** This form of leadership recognizes the value of participation and collaboration. Leaders encourage active involvement of team members in decision-making, fostering a sense of belonging and engagement.

5. **Ethical Leadership:** While ethics has always played a role in leadership, the emphasis on ethical leadership underscores the importance of

moral principles and justice in decision-making and guiding actions.

6. **Relational Leadership:** This approach views leadership not as a series of traits or behaviors of an individual but as a relational dynamic between leaders and followers. It focuses on interactions and building meaningful relationships.

With the evolution of society and global challenges such as sustainability, inclusion and diversity, and digitalization, new leadership models are likely to emerge. What is clear is that leadership is not static; it evolves in response to the needs, challenges, and opportunities of the moment. Contemporary leadership theories acknowledge the complexity and nuance required to lead in a rapidly changing world.

Continuing the discussion on contemporary leadership theories, we can explore further aspects and facets of these approaches. The role of technology has had a significant impact on contemporary leadership. With the advent of social media, digitalization, and globalization, leaders must now operate in multi-channel and cross-functional environments. This has led to the emergence of what we might call "digital leadership," where the ability to communicate effectively through digital platforms and understand the dynamics of new media has become essential.

1. The Importance of Diversity and Inclusion: Alongside this, the significance of diversity and inclusion in contemporary leadership cannot be underestimated. Organizations are increasingly recognizing the value of having diverse teams and leadership that reflects this diversity. Inclusive leadership goes beyond mere acceptance of differences; it requires actively valuing these differences and a commitment to creating environments where everyone feels valued and heard.

2. Adaptive Leadership: Another concept emerging is that of adaptive leadership. In a rapidly changing world where challenges arise in unpredictable ways, leaders must have the ability to adapt and respond with flexibility. This requires not only a deep understanding of the external context but also the capacity for self-reflection and internal change.

3. Holistic Leadership: Holistic leadership is another concept gaining ground. This approach considers the whole being – mind, body, and spirit – in the context of leadership. Mental health, physical well-being, and spiritual balance are seen as crucial components for an effective and resilient leader.

4. Neuroscience and Leadership: With the emergence of neuroscience, we are beginning to better understand how the brain relates to leadership. Some research suggests that there are specific parts of the brain involved in decision-making, empathy, and problem-solving – all crucial skills for leaders. This understanding is driving new approaches to leadership training and development.

5. Sustainability in Leadership: Finally, we cannot ignore the growing interest in sustainability in leadership. Contemporary leaders are increasingly called upon to consider the long-term impact of their decisions, not only in terms of financial results but also in terms of environmental, social, and cultural impact.

Leadership is evolving in response to a myriad of internal and external factors. In this complex landscape, a leader's ability to stay updated, learn continuously, and demonstrate resilience becomes increasingly critical.

In today's landscape, leadership is moving beyond the traditional boundaries of organizations and business to touch almost every aspect of daily life and society. This has led to the evolution of several new models and paradigms.

Distributed Leadership: The concept of "Distributed Leadership" has become particularly relevant in flat organizations and ad-hoc structures. Instead of a single individual at the helm, leadership responsibility is distributed among various people or groups within an organization. This can help leverage the diverse skills and experiences of team members and create more resilient leadership.

Collaborative Leadership: In parallel, there has been growing recognition of the importance of "Collaborative Leadership." This model emphasizes collaboration between leaders and team members, involving everyone in defining the vision and decision-making. This leadership style can be particularly effective in complex and rapidly evolving environments, where agility and responsiveness are crucial.

Resilient Leadership: The concept of "Resilient Leadership" is another emerging paradigm. In a world where crises, both big and small, seem to be the norm rather than the exception, a leader's ability to withstand, adapt, and thrive in the face of adversity is fundamental. This requires a deep understanding of oneself, one's emotional reactions, and coping mechanisms, as well as the ability to view challenges as opportunities rather than threats.

Cultural Leadership: Alongside this, "Cultural Leadership" is gaining increasing attention. In a globalized world, leaders often need to navigate through diverse cultures, be they national, organizational, or team-based. Understanding and appreciating these cultural differences, and knowing how to use them to create synergies rather than conflicts, is a key competency for contemporary leaders.

Mindful Leadership: Another emerging trend is the interest in "Mindful Leadership." Inspired by mindfulness and meditation practices, this form of leadership emphasizes presence, awareness, and attention to the present moment. These leaders are attuned to their feelings, thoughts, and behaviors, as well as those of the people around them, leading to more thoughtful decisions and authentic relationships.

Augmented Leadership: Finally, the advent of artificial intelligence and robotics is also influencing leadership theories. The role of the "Augmented Leader" – where human capabilities are amplified through technology – is becoming increasingly relevant. While some decision-making functions can be automated, the human ability to show empathy, understand nuances, and build deep relationships cannot be easily replicated by a machine. Therefore, even in this highly technological environment, "human" skills remain at the core of effective leadership.

Contemporary leadership theories represent a rich and varied mosaic of ideas and approaches, all deeply rooted in the context of the 21st century. They share the common understanding that traditional models of leadership, while important, are not always adequate to address the rapidly evolving challenges of today's world.

Starting with "Distributed Leadership," we have seen how modern organizations often disperse decision-making authority across various levels, rather than centralizing it in a single individual or group. This distribution not only leverages the variety of skills within an organization but also encourages innovation and agility.

On the other hand, "Collaborative Leadership" emphasizes the importance of building a shared vision, where leaders work closely with their teams, fostering greater engagement and responsibility. This model recognizes that optimal solutions often emerge from collectivity rather than from a single individual.

At the same time, "Resilient Leadership" highlights the importance of tenacity and adaptability. In an era of uncertainty and rapid change, leaders must not only have a clear vision but also the resilience to pursue it, regardless of the obstacles they may encounter along the way.

The concepts of "Cultural Leadership" and "Mindful Leadership," on the other hand, acknowledge that today's leaders must navigate a nuanced landscape, ranging from cultural differences to emotional complexity. The ability to be fully present, show empathy, and understand diverse perspectives has become crucial.

In conclusion, it is important to emphasize that, while there are many contemporary theories and models, effective leadership is not reducible to a single formula or approach. Leadership is a journey of continuous growth and learning. Successful leaders of the 21st century will be those who combine lessons from the past with a deep understanding of the challenges and opportunities of the present and who are ready to evolve and adapt in response to an unpredictable future. In other words, contemporary leadership is as much an art as it is a science and requires a blend of intuition, understanding, courage, and, above all, the ability to authentically connect with others.

6. Leadership and Power: Types of Power and How They Are Exercised by Leaders.

Power in leadership refers to the ability to influence the behavior of others, both through formal and informal mechanisms. Understanding the various types of power and how they are exercised by leaders is essential for interpreting and effectively guiding organizational dynamics. Here is a breakdown of the various types of power and how they are typically exercised in leadership:

1. Legitimate Power:

    - Definition: Derives from one's formal position or title within an organization.

    - Example of use: A manager may assign specific tasks to a team member based on their official role.

2. Coercive Power:

- Definition: Relies on the ability to punish or inflict some form of harm.

- Example of use: A leader may threaten to terminate or demotivate an employee if they fail to meet certain performance standards.

3. Reward Power:

- Definition: Involves the ability to provide rewards or incentives.

- Example of use: A leader may offer a bonus or promotion as an incentive for an employee's excellent performance.

4. Referent Power:

- Definition: Relies on personal attraction and charisma. People follow the leader because they admire or respect them.

- Example of use: A charismatic leader may motivate their team through inspirational speeches and by creating an emotional bond.

5. Expert Power:

- Definition: Derives from expertise, skills, and knowledge in a particular field.

- Example of use: In a research and development team, an expert in a specific area may lead a project because of their technical skills respected by others.

6. Informational Power:

- Definition: Is based on having information that others deem valuable.

- Example of use: A team member who is the sole possessor of project details may use this information as leverage to influence decisions.

Each type of power has its place within organizations, and effective leaders often use a combination of these powers depending on the situation. However, it is crucial for leaders to be aware of the ethical implications when exercising power. Abuse of power, especially coercive power, can have detrimental effects on organizational culture and employee trust. Therefore, credibility and integrity are paramount when exercising any form of power in a leadership context.

As established, power is the ability to influence the behavior of others. In a leadership context, this power can be exercised in various ways and can originate from different sources. The relationship between leadership and power is not always linear and can vary depending on culture, context, and the people involved.

The psychology of power is an intriguing aspect. Studies have shown that those who hold power tend to have a more optimistic and positive outlook, often making assertive decisions. Conversely, those who perceive themselves as lacking power tend to display more caution in their decisions. Therefore, the perception of power has a significant impact on how people act and react in different situations.

Furthermore, how a leader perceives and uses power can have profound implications for group dynamics. For example, leaders who overly rely on coercive power may create a toxic work environment where employees act out of fear rather than intrinsic motivation. On the other hand, a leader who can balance rewarding and referent power can build a positive and motivating workplace.

The distribution of power is another crucial aspect. In some organizations, power is highly centralized, with one individual or a small group holding most of the decision-making control. In other contexts, power is distributed, allowing various team members or organization members to have a say in decisions. This distribution can influence the speed of decision-making, innovation, and employee satisfaction.

Another interesting facet is the relationship between power and responsibility. As the famous saying goes, "With great power comes great responsibility," leaders must be aware of the consequences of their actions. This awareness can help prevent abuses of power and ensure that decisions are made in the best interest of all stakeholders.

A leader should also be aware of the concept of "soft" power or informal power. This refers to influences that are not tied to formal positions or tangible resources but rather to relationships, reputation, and charisma. Often, individuals with significant "soft" power can exert considerable influence even without a formal leadership position.

In summary, while leadership and power are closely linked concepts, their relationship is complex and multifaceted. An effective leader not only recognizes the different types of power at their disposal but also understands the nuances and implications of each, acting with integrity and awareness.

The intersection of leadership and power extends well beyond the traditional types of power listed above. The evolution of leadership over time has seen new dynamics and challenges related to the exercise of power, and these challenges have become particularly relevant in the modern era.

Power Through Networks: In today's interconnected world, leaders can no longer rely solely on traditional hierarchical power. The ability to build and maintain professional and personal networks has gained new importance. These networks can act as power amplifiers, providing leaders with access to information, resources, and influences beyond their traditional spheres.

Cultural Power: Globalization has led organizations to operate in culturally diverse contexts. Leaders must now navigate and respect cultural differences, recognizing that what is powerful and influential in one culture may not be so in another. A leader's ability to understand and adapt to these differences can determine the success or failure of their initiatives.

Power and Ethics: The link between power and ethics has become central in contemporary leadership discussions. Leaders today are subject to intense public scrutiny, and any abuse of power can have immediate and lasting repercussions. This has led to a greater emphasis on ethics and integrity in leadership.

Power and Vulnerability: Contrary to what one might think, showing vulnerability can actually empower a leader. Admitting mistakes, seeking feedback, and being open to learning can strengthen the trust and loyalty of followers. In a way, vulnerability can become a source of authentic power.

Power and Listening: One often overlooked aspect of power is the ability to listen actively. Leaders who genuinely listen to the concerns, ideas, and feedback of their teams are often seen as more legitimate and influential. Listening can provide the leader with valuable information that may not be otherwise accessible.

Power and Innovation: In an era dominated by the speed of change and technological revolution, the ability to innovate has become a key source of power. Leaders who can drive innovation and adapt quickly to changes have a significant advantage over competitors.

Power and Self-Awareness: A leader who deeply understands their strengths, weaknesses, motivations, and values is better equipped to exercise power effectively and ethically. Self-awareness can also help leaders prevent the abuse of power by offering a form of internal control over their actions.

In any case, while power is an essential tool in a leader's toolkit, how it is used can define the true nature and effectiveness of that leadership.

The realm of leadership and power is vast and varied, with countless nuances and perspectives to consider. Here are further insights:

Power and Emotional Intelligence: Emotional intelligence is the ability to recognize, understand, and manage one's own emotions and to recognize, understand, and influence the emotions of others. This competence is crucial for exercising effective power. Leaders with high emotional intelligence tend to have deeper relationships, communicate better, and resolve conflicts more effectively.

Power and Storytelling: Stories have inherent power. Leaders who can build and tell persuasive stories can shape an organization's culture, influence perceptions, and motivate teams. Storytelling can be used to instill vision, values, and direction.

Power and Legitimacy: It is not enough to hold power; it must be perceived as legitimate by followers. The legitimacy of power can come from various sources: a formal position, respect earned through actions, or the approval of authoritative external figures. Legitimacy can establish or erode trust in leadership.

Power and Resilience: A leader's ability to withstand, recover from, and thrive in the face of challenges is essential. Resilience can be seen as a form of inner power, providing leaders with the strength and determination to overcome obstacles.

Power and Decision-Making: The ability to make decisions, large or small, lies at the heart of exercising power. But it's not just about deciding; it's also about how decisions are made, communicated, and implemented. Transparency, inclusivity, and consideration in decision-making can strengthen the perception of legitimate power.

Power and Vision: Vision is the ability to see the big picture, imagine a desirable future, and inspire others to work toward that future. A clear and compelling vision can serve as a powerful means of influencing and mobilizing people.

Power and Adaptability: Today's world is constantly changing. A leader's ability to adapt to new circumstances, learn from experiences, and navigate uncertainty is essential. Adaptability can also influence how power is exercised and perceived in fluid situations.

Power and Delegation: While it's essential for a leader to be competent and informed, it's equally crucial to recognize when to delegate. Effective delegation can empower people, distribute responsibility, and maximize an organization's resources.

Conclusion: Leadership and Power The relationship between leadership and power is complex, multifaceted, and fundamental to understanding the essence of a leader's role. The ability to exercise power in ways that are effective, ethical, and respectful is at the heart of successful leadership.

Initially, it might be tempting to consider power as a simple lever that a leader can pull to achieve results. However, as we have seen, power is much more than that. It interacts with a wide range of skills, behaviors, circumstances, and challenges. From recognizing the importance of emotional intelligence to the ability to narrate and motivate, to the need for adaptability and resilience, power is not a static entity but rather a dynamic force.

Some leaders fall into the trap of relying too much on the power conferred by their position. But power tied exclusively to position is fragile. True power, the kind that inspires trust and loyalty, stems from a leader's integrity, competence, empathy, and their ability to serve the common good. Effective delegation, active listening, and the ability to make informed and considerate decisions are all elements that reinforce the positive nature of a leader's power.

Furthermore, in a globalized and interconnected world, power can no longer be wielded in isolation. Leaders must consider the cultural, ethical, and social implications of their actions. The legitimacy of power, as we have noted, is crucial. Without the perception of legitimacy, a leader's power can quickly become contradictory or, in the worst cases, harmful.

Ultimately, it is essential for leaders to be aware of the various sources and types of power at their disposal and to navigate among them with wisdom and discernment. Power, when used well, can be a force for good, guiding organizations toward common goals, inspiring innovation and progress, and creating an environment where individuals feel valued and motivated.

In conclusion, while leadership and power are closely related concepts, it is the depth of understanding, the wisdom in application, and integrity in behavior that truly define great leaders. They recognize that power is not an end in itself but a tool to achieve a greater vision, serve others, and make a positive impact in the world.

7. Culture and Leadership: How Different Cultures Influence Leadership Styles and Expectations Culture and Leadership: How Different Cultures Influence Leadership Styles and Expectations Culture is the set of values, beliefs, practices, and norms that define a society or organization. It has a profound and pervasive influence on how people think, behave, and interact. Leadership is not immune to this influence. Expectations, perceptions, and leadership styles can vary significantly from one culture to another, and understanding these differences is crucial for global leaders and anyone operating in multicultural contexts.

Cultural Values and Leadership: Each culture has a set of values that are considered important and desirable. For example, while some cultures value individualism and competition, others may emphasize community, collaboration, and harmony. These values directly influence what is considered an effective or acceptable leadership style.

Role Expectations: In some cultures, leaders are expected to be authoritative decision-makers, while in others, they may be seen as facilitators or mediators. These expectations can determine how a leader is perceived and how successful they can be in guiding a group or organization.

Communication: Communication is fundamental in leadership, and each culture has its norms regarding it. While some cultures value direct and clear communication, others may prefer more subtle and indirect communication. Leaders must be aware of these differences to avoid misunderstandings and conflicts.

Conflict Management: Cultures also vary in how they perceive and manage conflicts. While some cultures see conflict as something to be avoided, others accept it as a natural part of human interactions and an opportunity for growth and learning.

Power Perception: In some cultures, power distances are emphasized, and significant differences between leaders and followers are expected. In others, greater equality and collaboration between leaders and teams are anticipated.

Decision-Making Approaches: In some cultures, decisions are made in a top-down manner, with leaders making choices for the group. In others, participation and consensus are prioritized, and decisions often result from extensive discussions and group deliberations.

Ethics and Integrity: Cultural norms can also influence expectations regarding ethics and integrity in leadership. What is considered ethical in one culture may not be so in another, and leaders must be careful when navigating these complex waters.

It is clear that culture has a profound impact on leadership. Leaders who want to succeed in multicultural contexts must be culturally intelligent, capable of recognizing and respecting cultural differences, and ready to adapt their style and approach accordingly. In a globalized world, the ability to understand and navigate the complexities of culture and leadership is more crucial than ever.

Culture and Leadership: Further Reflections
Mutual Influence of Culture and Leadership:
While culture influences leadership, leadership can
also influence and shape culture. A charismatic or
influential leader can introduce new values or norms
that later become integral to organizational or societal
culture. This bidirectional dynamic makes the
relationship between culture and leadership
particularly interesting and complex.

Multicultural Leaders: With the advent of
globalization, leaders have emerged who embody more
than one culture. These leaders can draw from a variety
of cultural contexts, synthesizing them into a unique
and hybrid leadership approach. This ability to "code-
switch" or switch between different cultural modes can
be a tremendous advantage in a global environment.

Ceremonies and Rituals: Every culture has its own
ceremonies and rituals, which can have significant
symbolic roles. These rituals can hold deep meaning
for members of that culture and can serve to reinforce
a leader's authority and legitimacy. Ignoring or
downplaying these rituals can lead to a loss of respect
or credibility for a leader.

Cultural Learning Methodologies: Intercultural
training has become a fundamental component of
leadership development. This can include everything
from learning languages to familiarizing oneself with

cultural norms and etiquettes, to immersion in a culture through travel or extended overseas experiences. This type of training can help leaders develop intercultural sensitivity and understanding.

Bias and Stereotypes: While cultural awareness is essential, it is also crucial for leaders to recognize and challenge their own biases and stereotypes. Operating on unverified assumptions or preconceived ideas about a particular culture can lead to judgment errors or misunderstandings. Personal reflection and self-examination are key tools in this context.

Spiritual and Religious Leadership: In many cultures, spirituality and religion are deeply intertwined with social norms and values. This can influence leadership expectations and perceptions of authority. Religious leaders, for example, can have a significant influence on social, political, and even economic issues within a specific community or nation.

Gender Dynamics and Leadership: Culture can also influence perceptions and expectations regarding gender roles in leadership. In some cultures, female leaders may face particular challenges or barriers to entry into positions of power, while in others, they may have access to specific opportunities and support.

Adaptation Techniques: Adapting to different cultures does not necessarily mean losing one's identity or leadership style. Often, it involves learning how to present one's ideas in a way that resonates with the local culture or understanding the communicative or behavioral nuances that can make a difference.

Every culture carries a unique treasure of experiences, stories, and lessons. Successful leaders know how to draw from these resources, learn from them, and use them to build bridges, create understanding, and lead with empathy and vision.

Global and Local Influences in Leadership Glocalization: This term blends "global" and "local," emphasizing the importance of combining global visions with local sensitivities. "Glocal" leadership entails the need to operate on a global scale while maintaining a deep understanding of local realities. For example, a multinational corporation may seek to expand its presence in a new country, but to succeed, it must understand and respect the cultural and market specificities of the place.

Digitalization and Culture: Technology has made the world more interconnected than ever before. With the advent of social media, video conferencing platforms, and other technologies, people from diverse cultures can communicate and interact in ways that were not possible before. This interconnectedness has led to a sort of global "digital culture" with its own norms and expectations. Leaders must understand how this digital culture interacts with local cultures and how it can be used to enhance their leadership.

Organizational Culture vs. National Culture: While we discuss culture in terms of nations or ethnicities, we must not forget the powerful influence of organizational culture. Organizations have their own cultures, which can sometimes be in contrast or in harmony with national cultures. Understanding this dynamic is crucial for any leader seeking to influence an organization.

Language and Leadership: Each language carries a certain mindset and worldview. Some languages have words or concepts that do not exist in other languages. These linguistic nuances can influence communication, decision-making, and conflict resolution. A leader's ability to speak or understand different languages, or at least to have awareness of linguistic subtleties, can be a significant advantage.

Education and Cultural Training: Education plays a crucial role in shaping a person's cultural outlook and expectations. Leaders who have had educational experiences in different parts of the world or in multicultural environments often bring a broader perspective and greater flexibility to their leadership abilities.

Group Dynamics and Cultural Identity: Within a culture, there may be subgroups or minorities with their unique norms and expectations. Leaders must recognize these dynamics and ensure they do not make overly broad generalizations or assumptions about a culture based solely on the dominant majority.

Traditions and Innovation: While cultures have their established traditions and practices, they are also capable of change and innovation. Leaders must balance respect for traditions with an acknowledgment of the need and desire for innovation and progress.

The dance between culture and leadership is intricate and complex, full of challenges but also immense opportunities. In an increasingly interconnected world, a leader's ability to cross cultural boundaries with empathy, respect, and understanding will be increasingly valuable.

The relationship between culture and leadership is invaluable and complex. This connection is rooted in the history of humanity and manifests in every aspect of our social and organizational behavior.

1. The Interplay of Culture and Identity: Culture is not merely a set of customs, languages, or traditions; it is the lens through which we view the world and define our identity. Similarly, leadership is not just about guidance and direction; it is also a manifestation of values, beliefs, and visions. Therefore, how a leader interprets and acts in their role is profoundly influenced by their culture of origin and the culture of the community or organization they lead.

2. A Global Vision, Local Application: In an era of globalization, a leader may have a vision that transcends national borders. However, the ability to adapt this vision to local realities while respecting cultural particularities is what distinguishes successful leaders. "Glocalization" thus becomes a crucial skill.

3. The Responsibility of Understanding: Being aware of cultural differences is not enough; understanding them is essential. Cultural misunderstandings can lead to conflicts, inefficiencies, and missed opportunities. Leaders must take responsibility for educating themselves and their teams about these differences and how to navigate them successfully.

4. Balancing Tradition and Innovation: While tradition provides stability and continuity, innovation drives progress. Leaders must know how to honor cultural traditions while encouraging the adoption of new ideas and approaches, finding a balance between respecting the past and envisioning the future.

5. Multicultural Dynamics: Multicultural teams can offer a unique blend of skills, perspectives, and solutions. However, they can also present challenges in terms of communication, integration, and cohesion. An effective leader recognizes and values diversity, promoting an environment where every member feels respected, heard, and valued.

6. Continuous Growth: Intercultural learning is not a goal to achieve but a path of continuous growth. The world changes, cultures evolve, and new dynamics emerge. A leader should remain an eternal student of culture, always seeking to broaden their understanding and adaptability.

In summary, culture and leadership are inherently linked. They influence each other in ways that can be subtle or overt. In today's globalized society, the ability to integrate these two dimensions with empathy, insight, and flexibility has become more crucial than ever. Leaders who recognize the importance of this interconnection and actively work to cultivate it are the ones who will thrive in the ever-evolving global landscape.

8. Female Leadership: The Importance and Uniqueness of Female Leadership in the Modern Context. In recent decades, female leadership has emerged as a significant field of study and a practical reality in many societies and organizations worldwide. Although women have always held leadership roles in various contexts, the increasing presence and acceptance of female leadership in business, politics, and society deserve special attention.

1. History and Background: Despite historical and cultural barriers, many women have emerged as leaders in various fields over the centuries. Figures like Cleopatra, Joan of Arc, and Queen Elizabeth I are historical examples, but even in the 20th and 21st centuries, figures like Indira Gandhi, Angela Merkel, and Jacinda Ardern have demonstrated women's ability to lead nations and address global challenges.

2. Collaborative and Inclusive Leadership: A distinctive characteristic often associated with female leadership is a collaborative and inclusive approach. Many female leaders tend to value teamwork, consultation, and inclusion rather than adopting autocratic or top-down leadership styles.

3. Empathy and Emotional Intelligence: Some studies suggest that women may, on average, have higher emotional intelligence than men. This ability to understand and connect with others' emotions can translate into more empathetic leadership, which, in turn, can lead to more cohesive and motivated teams.

4. Multitasking and Holistic Management: Women are often praised for their multitasking abilities and their capacity to see the "big picture." This holistic view can aid in the effective management of complex projects and consideration of various stakeholders.

5. Challenges and Barriers: Despite progress, women leaders still face many challenges, including gender stereotypes, discrimination, and the glass ceiling. These barriers may require women to develop resilience, determination, and adaptability, qualities that can further enrich their leadership style.

6. The Importance of Diversity: Gender diversity in leadership leads to greater diversity of ideas, approaches, and solutions. Numerous studies have shown that organizations with balanced gender leadership tend to perform better both financially and in terms of employee satisfaction.

7. Role Models: Female leaders serve as role models not only for other women but for society as a whole. They demonstrate that gender should not be a barrier to success or the ability to positively influence the world.

8. Future Vision: As the world continues to evolve and global challenges become increasingly complex, female leadership will be essential in bringing diverse perspectives, innovative approaches, and sustainable solutions to the forefront.

Female Leadership and Social Impact

In the socio-cultural context, female leadership has a profound impact. Women leaders, through their personal and professional stories, challenge existing gender norms and sometimes break barriers limiting women in many sectors of society.

Communication Styles: Communication is central to leadership, and many women leaders are distinguished by their communication style. They tend to use more collaborative and inclusive language, emphasizing active listening. This communication style can facilitate bridge-building, negotiation, and mediation – essential skills in complex contexts.

Female Leadership and Innovation: Contrary to some stereotypes, women leaders are often at the forefront of innovation. Whether in technology, science, art, or business, women leaders bring new perspectives and ideas that can catalyze change and drive entire sectors in previously unexplored directions.

Education and Growth: In many contexts, women leaders emphasize the importance of education as a means of empowerment. Many female leaders come from backgrounds where access to education was limited, and as a result, they emphasize the need to provide educational opportunities, especially to girls and young women.

Balancing Work and Personal Life: Women leaders are often at the center of discussions about work-life balance. While this is an issue for leaders of all genders, women, given socio-cultural expectations regarding gender roles, must navigate unique challenges. Their experiences in this regard can provide valuable lessons on how to manage the pressures of leadership while maintaining a balance in personal life.

Networking and Mentorship: Building networks and mentorship are essential for professional growth. Many women leaders recognize the importance of having mentors and, in turn, become mentors for the next generation. These relationships not only help develop skills and capabilities but also create a sense of belonging and community.

Resilience and Perseverance: Given the numerous challenges women face when ascending the leadership ladder, resilience is a quality many female leaders possess in abundance. This resilience is not just the ability to withstand pressure but also to adapt and thrive in the face of adversity.

Ethics and Values: Finally, many women leaders place ethics and values at the core of their leadership. Whether it's sustainability, social justice, or equity, women leaders tend to have a strong moral compass that guides their decisions and actions.

The rise of women in leadership positions is not only a sign of progress in terms of gender equity but also brings a myriad of benefits and lessons for society as a whole. The uniqueness of female leadership enriches the fabric of organizations and communities and provides a variety of approaches and solutions to the challenges of the modern world.

The Role of Women Leaders in Non-Profit Organizations

Women leaders have shown a particular propensity for the non-profit sector, bringing passion, empathy, and a vision oriented toward social impact. In this context, they often address issues related to human rights, education, health, and community well-being. A collaborative approach and the ability to build relationships are fundamental in these sectors, and many women leaders excel in these areas, bridging different organizations and communities to maximize social impact.

Female Leadership in Science and Technology

Despite historical barriers, women leaders are emerging as prominent figures in scientific and technological fields. From scientists to CEOs of technology companies, women are challenging stereotypes and demonstrating that competence and innovation know no gender. In these roles, women often bring a different sensitivity to ethical issues, especially when it comes to innovations that have a direct impact on people.

Social Influence and Media

In the world of media and social influence, women leaders are shaping opinions and attitudes. From journalism to the entertainment industry, women in leadership positions influence how stories are told and interpreted. Their approach, often centered on authenticity and truth, can serve as a powerful counterpoint to narratives traditionally dominated by males.

Women Leaders and Politics

The global political scene has seen a significant increase in women in leadership positions, from prime ministers to presidents. These leaders not only bring a different perspective to seats of power but also influence policies to better reflect the needs of all citizens. Issues of equity, women's rights, education, and healthcare tend to receive greater attention when women are in decision-making positions.

The Importance of Role Models

The visibility of women in leadership positions serves as a model for younger generations. These role models show that women can aspire to any position or role in society, regardless of cultural or social obstacles. The presence of women leaders in various sectors can inspire girls and young women to pursue their passions and believe in their potential.

Female Leadership in the Business World

Even in the private sector, women leaders are making their presence felt. While there are still barriers to overcome, many women are now at the helm of major multinational corporations, innovative startups, and small businesses. These female leaders not only guide their companies to financial success but also emphasize the importance of sustainability, corporate ethics, and social responsibility.

Female Leadership: A Growing Force in the Global Landscape

Female leadership has taken on an increasingly prominent role over the past few decades. This not only reflects a cultural and social shift but also signifies the emergence of a new dynamic in how organizations and societies operate. The combination of skills, empathy, resilience, and a unique perspective makes female leadership a powerful and indispensable force in the contemporary landscape.

Toward Balanced Leadership

Despite progress, barriers persist. Gender pay inequity, gender-based discrimination, and limited access to leadership positions are still issues that many women face daily. However, it is important to note that female leadership is not solely a matter of gender but represents a balanced approach to management and decision-making that considers a variety of perspectives and experiences.

Innovative Contributions

Women leaders have demonstrated their ability to make innovative contributions in a wide range of sectors, from those traditionally dominated by men, such as technology and science, to areas where they have always had a presence, such as education and healthcare. Their ability to collaborate, build relationships, and consider holistic aspects of issues makes them particularly adept at navigating complex and interconnected contexts.

Cultural and Social Influence

The presence of women in leadership positions also has a profound impact on cultural and social evolution. It offers new role models, challenges gender stereotypes, and promotes a more inclusive and diversified view of success. This, in turn, contributes to creating fairer, more balanced, and resilient societies.

The Road Ahead

Although female leadership has achieved significant milestones, the path to full equality and inclusion is still long. It is essential to continue supporting and promoting women in leadership positions, ensuring that they have the resources, opportunities, and support needed to thrive. Only then can we hope for a world where leadership truly represents the diversity and richness of human experiences.

In conclusion, while the concept of female leadership may have started as a subtheme of the broader leadership discussion, today it represents a field of study and practice in its own right. Its importance in shaping the future of organizations and societies cannot be underestimated.

Challenges of Leadership: Conflict Management, Active Listening, Empathy, and Resilience

Every leader, regardless of their position, industry, or background, faces a set of challenges inherent to the leadership role. These challenges are often amplified by the complex dynamics of modern organizations, the ever-changing nature of work, and the rising expectations of employees and other stakeholders. Let's explore some of these key challenges and why they are crucial in the context of leadership.

1. Conflict Management:

Conflict management is one of the primary challenges for every leader. Every organization consists of individuals with diverse opinions, values, experiences, and expectations. This diversity can lead to disagreements and tensions.

- **Complexity:** In a work environment, conflicts can arise for various reasons, ranging from disagreements on business decisions to interpersonal tensions to power struggles.

- **Required Competence:** An effective leader must be able to identify the source of conflict, facilitate open communication between involved parties, and guide the team toward a constructive resolution.

2. Active Listening:

Active listening goes beyond merely hearing what is said. It involves truly understanding, interpreting, and evaluating what is heard.

- **Challenging in Noisy Environments:** In fast-paced and noisy organizations, it can be difficult for leaders to pause and genuinely listen to what others are trying to communicate.

- **Critical for Inclusion:** Without active listening, team members may feel overlooked or misunderstood, leading to reduced morale and productivity.

3. Empathy:

Empathy is the ability to understand and share the feelings of another. It is crucial for building authentic and trust-based relationships.

- **Challenging in Results-Oriented Environments:** In organizations heavily focused on results, it can be challenging for leaders to pause and consider the emotions and individual needs of team members.

- **Impact on Organizational Culture:** Lack of empathy can lead to a cold or distant organizational culture, where employees feel like mere cogs rather than valued members of a team.

4. Resilience:

Resilience is the ability to adapt and recover quickly from difficulties. It is essential for addressing unexpected changes and challenges in the business environment.

- **Challenges in Rapidly Changing Contexts:** With the rapid pace of technological and market changes, leaders need to be resilient to guide their teams through periods of uncertainty.

- **Balancing Resilience and Flexibility:**
  Striking a balance between maintaining a clear
  vision and adapting to new information or
  circumstances is an ongoing challenge for
  leaders.

In conclusion, while technical skills and industry
experience are certainly important for a leader, it is the
ability to navigate these interpersonal and
organizational challenges that often determines a
leader's success. Developing and refining these skills —
conflict management, active listening, empathy, and
resilience — is crucial for any leader aspiring to have a
lasting and positive impact on their organization.

Adapting to Evolving Leadership Challenges

The management of challenges inherent in leadership
is an evolving task. In addition to the points already
outlined, such as conflict management, active listening,
empathy, and resilience, further considerations emerge
depending on contexts, circumstances, and
organizational cultures. These factors often intertwine,
creating more complex scenarios that require leaders
to exhibit greater flexibility and sensitivity.

Managing Expectations:

One of the challenges is managing expectations. Leaders and team members may have divergent expectations regarding outcomes, processes, and relationships. Misalignment of expectations can lead to disappointments and disagreements. An effective leader must be skilled at managing and aligning expectations through clear and consistent communication. This skill is closely tied to active listening, as truly understanding others' expectations often requires careful listening.

Change Management:

Furthermore, change management is a persistent challenge in leadership. Changes can be driven by various factors, such as technological innovations, market competition, or internal developments. Leaders must be able to guide their teams through transitional phases, often in the face of resistance. This requires a combination of empathy to understand the team's fears and concerns and resilience to stay focused on long-term goals.

Building and Maintaining Organizational Culture:

Another aspect is the construction and maintenance of organizational culture. Every organization has its own culture, which can range from highly hierarchical to more horizontal and collaborative. Organizational culture is largely shaped by the leader's behavior and expectations. This means that every action, decision, or communication by the leader can have a significant impact on the organization's culture. A toxic culture can hinder innovation, lower morale, and reduce productivity, so a leader must be highly aware of the impact they can have.

Managing Diversity:

Managing diversity is also a significant challenge. Diverse teams can bring a variety of perspectives and solutions to problems but can also lead to misunderstandings and tensions. A leader's ability to value diversity and incorporate a wide range of viewpoints is closely related to their capacity for empathy and active listening.

Ethical Responsibility:

Additionally, the issue of ethical responsibility is increasingly in the spotlight. With growing awareness of social, environmental, and governance issues, leaders are more frequently under pressure to act ethically and responsibly. This not only requires a solid understanding of ethical matters but also the ability to act as role models and positively influence ethical culture within the organization.

These and many other challenges make up a complex framework that every leader must navigate. Each challenge can manifest in various degrees and forms, often overlapping and interacting in unexpected ways. Being an effective leader, therefore, is not just a matter of having a defined set of skills or following a series of steps; it is an ongoing process of learning, adapting, and growing.

Significant Aspects of Modern Leadership Challenges

A significant aspect of leadership challenges concerns the ability to adapt to new technologies. We live in an era where digitization, automation, and Artificial Intelligence are rapidly transforming the world of work. These innovations require leaders not only to understand new technologies but also to guide their teams through the adoption and integration of such technologies into existing processes. This can entail resistance from team members who may feel threatened by new technologies or lack the necessary skills to adapt.

Another challenge for modern leaders is the management of employee well-being and mental health. Increased awareness of mental health and well-being in the workplace has placed a greater emphasis on the need for compassionate and understanding leaders. This means creating a work environment where people feel safe discussing their concerns and needs, and where there is adequate support for issues like stress, anxiety, or depression.

An emerging field is sustainability and corporate social responsibility. Consumers, now more than ever, are aware of the environmental and social impact of the companies they do business with. This has led to increased pressure on business leaders to ensure that their organizations are not only profitable but also ethically responsible. This involves making decisions that balance profit with societal and environmental impact, a challenge that can often present complex dilemmas.

Additionally, leadership in multicultural and globalized contexts has become a fundamental component of modern challenges. Leaders must now be able to operate and communicate effectively across diverse cultures, languages, and social norms. This requires a deep understanding of cultural differences as well as the ability to build bridges and find common ground in diverse contexts.

The increasing complexity of markets, the interconnectivity of economies, and the speed of communications have also made the ability to make quick but informed decisions more crucial than ever. Leaders must now be able to process vast amounts of information, identify trends, and make strategic decisions in short timeframes while ensuring that such decisions are based on solid data and are in the organization's long-term best interests.

Another consideration is the expectation of transparency. In an era where information is easily accessible and organizations are increasingly under the spotlight, leaders must be prepared to operate in an environment where transparency is expected and demanded. This can involve managing sensitive issues such as information disclosure, crisis management, or responding to public concerns.

Striking the Balance Between Authority and Humility

Lastly, there's the challenge of striking a balance between authority and humility. While leaders must exercise authority to make decisions and provide direction, it's equally important for them to display humility by acknowledging their mistakes and learning from feedback. Humility can help build trust and respect between leaders and their teams, creating a more collaborative and productive work environment.

Leadership as a Multifaceted Skill Set

Leadership, as a concept, is one of the most coveted skills, yet one of the most complex to perfect. Contemporary leadership challenges are multifaceted and interconnected, requiring leaders to develop a range of skills beyond merely the ability to lead or command.

Starting with conflict management, every leader should possess the necessary skills to navigate and resolve disagreements and tensions constructively. This doesn't just mean arbitrating disputes but creating an environment where differences are seen as opportunities for learning and growth rather than obstacles.

In parallel, active listening is a crucial component of effective communication. A leader who genuinely listens to the concerns, ideas, and opinions of their colleagues can make more informed decisions and foster a more inclusive work environment. This kind of listening goes beyond receiving information; it implies understanding, processing, and responding appropriately.

Empathy, in turn, is closely tied to active listening. Being empathetic means putting oneself in others' shoes, understanding their emotions, and perspectives. In a workplace context, empathy can help form deeper bonds with team members, improve morale, and even lead to more ethical and balanced business decisions.

Finally, resilience represents a leader's ability to stand firm in the face of adversity, learn from failures, and move forward despite obstacles. In a constantly changing business world, where crises can emerge unexpectedly, resilience is often what distinguishes successful companies from those that struggle to survive.

In conclusion, modern leadership isn't reducible to a single competence or skill; it's a combination of many interconnected skills that, when cultivated and put into practice, can lead to effective and innovative management. Leadership challenges may seem daunting, but addressing them with intentionality and commitment can result in significant personal and organizational growth.

11. Leadership and Ethics: The Moral Responsibility of Leaders and the Importance of Integrity

Leadership extends beyond the ability to lead and direct; it also entails a profound ethical responsibility. The role of leaders doesn't end with mere management or the achievement of organizational goals; it extends to safeguarding values, honesty, and integrity within their functions. This connection between leadership and ethics is fundamental in a world where trust in leadership is increasingly challenged by scandals, corruption, and unethical behavior.

The Nature of Moral Responsibility:

Leaders, given their position of influence, have an inherent responsibility to those they lead. Their position requires them to make decisions that can have significant impacts on the well-being, careers, and even lives of individuals. This profound responsibility implies a high moral standard. It's not just about doing what's right for the organization but doing what's right, period.

Integrity as the Foundation of Leadership:

Integrity is often seen as one of the most important and respected traits in a leader. An integral leader is consistent in their actions, values, methods, measures, and principles. This consistency builds trust, an essential component of effective leadership. Without integrity, trust can be quickly eroded, compromising the leader's ability to lead effectively.

The Role of the Ethical Code:

Many organizations adopt ethical codes to guide the behavior of their leaders and employees. These codes serve as a moral compass, outlining expected standards of behavior and providing a reference in case of ethical dilemmas. However, an ethical code is effective only when supported by an organizational culture that values ethics and integrity.

Difficult Decisions and Ethics:

Leaders often find themselves having to make difficult decisions that can have ethical implications. In these moments, a leader's true ethical nature is put to the test. Balancing the needs of the organization with those of employees, stakeholders, and society at large requires deep reflection and a commitment to ethics.

The Leader's Responsibility to Cultivate an Ethical Culture:

In addition to behaving ethically, leaders have a responsibility to cultivate an organizational culture that values and promotes ethics. This includes encouraging transparency, promoting accountability, and creating an environment where employees feel safe in reporting unethical behaviors.

The relationship between leadership and ethics goes beyond a simple list of principles to follow. Its fabric is closely interwoven with psychology, sociology, and even philosophy. When a leader operates within a context, the environment in which they act is permeated by their values and integrity. But how does all of this translate into everyday life?

Ethical Challenges in a Globalized World:

In an increasingly interconnected world, a leader's decisions in one corner of the globe can have repercussions thousands of kilometers away. Globalization has expanded the scope of leaders' responsibilities. It's no longer enough to be ethical in one's small environment; leaders must consider the ramifications of their actions on a global scale. This requires a deep understanding of diverse cultures, regulations, and societal expectations.

Digital Ethics:

With digitization and the information age, leaders face new ethical challenges. Data collection and usage, online privacy, information management, and the ethics of emerging technologies (such as artificial intelligence) are issues that contemporary leaders must address. The temptation to use technology for competitive advantage can conflict with the need to operate ethically.

The Short-Term vs. Long-Term Dilemma:

In many business environments, there's incessant pressure to produce short-term results. This pressure can drive some leaders to take shortcuts or make decisions that are advantageous in the short run but detrimental in the long run. An ethical leader must balance these pressures, keeping in mind both the immediate and future interests of their organization and stakeholders.

Ethical Training and Development:

If ethics is fundamental to leadership, then how is it cultivated in an individual? Ethical training and development should be an integral part of every leader's journey. This could include formal training, mentorship, discussions on ethical dilemmas, and learning from past experiences (both positive and negative).

Responsibility to Future Generations:

An ethical leader cares not only for the people directly under their guidance today but also for future generations. This is particularly evident when it comes to issues like environmental sustainability, where today's decisions can have an impact for decades or centuries to come.

The Leader's Role as a Role Model:

Last but not least, a leader should never underestimate the importance of their role as a role model. People closely observe what leaders do and often model their behavior based on what they see. If a leader acts with integrity, honesty, and transparency, they encourage others to do the same.

In summary, while the connection between leadership and ethics may seem clear on paper, in practice, it can become extremely complex. Today's leaders must navigate a continuously evolving landscape, balancing the needs of the present with responsibilities for the future.

The Role of Organizations in Promoting Ethical Leadership:

Although ultimate ethical responsibility rests with individual leaders, organizations play a crucial role in fostering an environment where ethics are valued. Implementing codes of conduct, ethical training, and establishing ethical committees are just a few initiatives that organizations can undertake. When an organization values ethics as a fundamental part of its DNA, it facilitates the growth of leaders who operate with integrity.

The Concept of 'Situational Ethics':

What is considered ethical in one situation isn't always the same in another. Leaders, especially those operating at an international level, often contend with 'situational ethics,' where ethical expectations vary depending on the context. While the temptation might be to fully adapt to local norms, a true ethical leader seeks a balance between respecting local norms and adhering to universal ethical principles.

The Connection Between Ethics and Trust:

Ethics and trust are inherently linked. When a leader acts with integrity and demonstrates ethical consistency, they earn the trust of those around them. This trust, in turn, can translate into loyalty, dedication, and a sense of belonging among team members. Conversely, when a leader engages in unethical actions, trust can quickly erode, harming the organizational culture.

Virtual Realities and Ethics:

With the growing popularity of virtual and augmented realities, leaders find themselves navigating new ethical territories. These virtual worlds can present unique dilemmas, such as defining what is real and virtual, the implications of actions in a virtual environment, and safeguarding privacy and identity in these spaces.

Ethics in Media and Leadership:

Today's leaders live under the constant scrutiny of the media. A single mistake or lapse in judgment can be widely publicized and criticized. This media pressure can influence ethical decisions, with leaders tempted to conceal mistakes or avoid accountability. However, a genuinely ethical leader recognizes the importance of transparency and accountability, even in high-pressure media situations.

The Ethics of Sustainability:

In addition to environmental sustainability, there is a growing awareness of the importance of social and economic sustainability. This translates into issues like fair wage practices, equitable working conditions, and creating a positive impact on local communities. Today's leaders must consider these factors when making decisions that affect not only their organization but society as a whole.

Self-Reflection and Ethical Growth:

Finally, for a leader, ethical growth is an ongoing journey that requires self-reflection. Recognizing one's biases, challenging one's beliefs, and constantly striving for improvement are all crucial aspects of this journey. Through self-reflection, a leader can strengthen their understanding of ethics and ensure they act with integrity in every situation.

Ethics isn't just a list of rules and principles; it represents the heart and soul of an organization and the people who lead it. Ethical leadership, therefore, assumes crucial relevance in the ecosystem of modern organizations and society at large.

The Essence of Ethics in Leadership:

Integrity and ethics go hand in hand. Integrity represents the consistency of actions, values, methods, measures, principles, expectations, and outcomes. It reflects an individual's honest authenticity. A leader, as a role model for many, must possess strong integrity, which, combined with firm ethical principles, guides every decision and action.

The Role of Organizations:

An organization's culture can significantly influence the ethical behavior of its members. Organizations with a strong ethical culture tend to support leaders in making the right choices, even when these may not be the most convenient. Training programs, clear codes of conduct, and ethical guidelines help solidify strong ethics within an organization.

Ethical Dilemmas and the Leader's Responsibility:

Every leader, regardless of their role or sector, faces ethical dilemmas. These can range from managing resources and conflicts to interacting with customers or defining business strategies. In every situation, a leader is called upon to weigh the moral implications of their actions and decide based on what is right, not just what is convenient or profitable.

Social Impact and Responsibility:

Ethical leadership goes beyond the organization alone. It has profound implications for society at large. Leaders influence the economy, the environment, communities, and people's lives. Their ability to make ethical decisions can have an impact far beyond the company's bottom line, affecting the entire social fabric.

The Long-Term Vision:

While the temptation might be to focus on short-term goals, an ethical leader always looks at the bigger picture. They recognize that decisions made today can have long-term consequences and strive to ensure that these decisions are sustainable and beneficial not only for the organization but also for society as a whole.

Conclusion:

In conclusion, ethical leadership represents a deep and ongoing commitment. It's not about choosing the ethical path when convenient but adhering to moral principles even when it's challenging. For leaders who truly engage in this journey, the benefits are not only tangible in terms of business success but also intangible, in the respect and trust earned from those around them. In a rapidly evolving world, where moral challenges may present themselves in ever-new forms, a leader's ability to remain true to solid ethical principles will be their most valuable compass.

11. Techniques and Tools: Tools and Techniques to Enhance Leadership Skills:

Improving one's leadership skills is an ongoing challenge that requires dedication, practice, and self-awareness. Various techniques and tools can help leaders refine their abilities and adapt to changes in the work and social context.

1. **Training and Workshops:** Participating in leadership training courses and seminars can offer valuable insights and advanced techniques. Formal training may cover topics such as communication, conflict management, and team development.

2. **Coaching and Mentoring:** An experienced coach or mentor can provide personalized guidance, helping leaders identify and address their specific areas of weakness and leverage their strengths.

3. **360-Degree Feedback:** This tool allows leaders to receive feedback from colleagues, superiors, and subordinates, offering a comprehensive view of their leadership style and areas for improvement.

4. **Reflection Journals:** Maintaining a journal of daily challenges, decisions made, and their consequences helps leaders reflect on their

actions and learn from their mistakes and successes.

5. **Role-Playing:** Simulating specific situations through role-playing can help leaders develop empathy, decision-making skills, and negotiation competencies.

6. **Personal SWOT Analysis:** Similar to analyzing an organization, leaders can perform a personal SWOT analysis, identifying Strengths, Weaknesses, Opportunities, and Threats related to their leadership capabilities.

7. **Books and Reading Material:** Numerous books offer insights into various aspects of leadership, from classic methods to modern concepts. Reading can broaden leaders' perspectives and provide new ideas and strategies.

8. Discussion Groups: Joining or forming discussion groups with other leaders or professionals provides an opportunity to share experiences, challenges, and solutions, promoting collaborative learning.

9. Technological Tools: Various apps and software are available that can assist leaders in improving their skills, from time management to project management and team communication.

10. Meditation and Mindfulness: These practices help develop mental presence, patience, and the ability to manage stress, all essential skills for effective leadership.

In the vast landscape of leadership development, there are multiple approaches that can be further explored, each of which can provide a unique and valuable perspective. Leadership is indeed an evolving discipline, and depending on needs and circumstances, new techniques and tools can emerge to address specific challenges.

11. Behavioral Analysis: Technologies like big data analysis are offering new ways to understand leaders' behaviors. Through behavioral analysis, it's possible to track patterns and trends in decisions and actions, providing a detailed perspective on how a leader reacts in different situations.

12. Continuous Feedback: Beyond traditional 360-degree feedback, many organizations are adopting continuous feedback platforms, where team members can provide real-time comments and suggestions. This allows leaders to adapt quickly and respond to team needs proactively.

13. Virtual Simulations: With the advent of virtual and augmented reality, leaders can now immerse themselves in simulations that replicate real-life scenarios, allowing them to test their skills in a safe and controlled environment.

14. Social Network Analysis: Understanding how information flows within an organization is crucial. Social network analysis tools map relationships among individuals and groups, showing how communication and influence spread.

15. Experiential Training: Instead of relying solely on theory, experiential training puts leaders in situations where they can learn by doing. Whether it's team-building excursions or real projects, experience-based learning can have a profound impact.

16. Succession Planning: Dedicated tools and software for succession planning can help leaders and organizations identify and groom future leaders, ensuring a smooth transition and leadership continuity.

17. Introspection Exercises: Techniques like "reflective writing" or "walking meditation" can help leaders connect with their inner thoughts, evaluating their motivations, fears, and aspirations.

18. Peer Learning: Peer-to-peer learning offers leaders the opportunity to learn directly from their colleagues, leveraging diverse experiences and perspectives within the organization.

19. Advanced Listening Techniques: Beyond active listening, there are numerous techniques, like empathetic listening or global listening, that can help leaders better and more deeply understand the people they interact with.

20. Biofeedback and Neurofeedback: These techniques harness technology to provide leaders with real-time information about their physical and mental reactions. For example, they can learn to recognize when they're under stress and adopt techniques to manage it.

21. Gamification: The use of playful elements in the business context has gained ground as a means to develop leadership skills. Through games, simulations, and challenges, leaders can hone their skills in a less formal and often more engaging environment.

22. Executive Coaching: Coaching is a solution-oriented approach to help leaders identify and overcome specific obstacles. Coaches can offer customized feedback, tools, and strategies tailored to individual needs.

23. Reverse Mentoring: Here, more senior or experienced leaders are paired with younger team members, often to gain a fresh perspective or learn skills related to new technologies.

24. Leadership Diaries: Keeping a diary of one's experiences, challenges, and reflections can be a powerful means of introspection and personal growth.

25. Leadership Networks: Joining groups or networks of leaders from various sectors can enrich one's understanding and provide diverse perspectives on leadership.

26. Cross-Functional Training: Exposure to different business functions can broaden leaders' understanding of business dynamics and help them develop a more holistic mindset.

27. Mastermind Groups: Groups of people who regularly come together to discuss challenges, share resources, and offer mutual support. These groups can offer a combination of brainstorming, learning, and peer-to-peer support.

28. Project-Based Learning: Engaging in real and tangible projects can provide leaders with a deep practical understanding of specific areas, allowing them to immediately apply what they've learned.

29. Personality Assessment Tools: Tests like the Myers-Briggs Type Indicator or the DiSC Assessment can provide leaders with deep insights into their behavioral tendencies and how they might interact with others.

30. Innovation Labs: These are spaces where leaders can experiment with new ideas, prototype solutions, and receive feedback in a low-risk environment.

31. Visualization Techniques: The ability to visualize successes, challenges, and potential solutions can be a powerful tool in a leader's toolkit. This practice can help clarify goals and chart paths to achieve them.

32. Mindfulness Training: Mindfulness helps leaders stay centered, present, and responsive rather than reactive. Being aware of their own emotions and reactions can aid in decision-making and stress management.

33. Immersive Workshops: These workshops are designed to fully immerse participants in a topic or challenge, often taking them away from their usual work environment to minimize distractions.

34. Change Management Training: In a rapidly changing world, leaders need to be equipped with tools and techniques to effectively manage and lead change.

These are just some of the countless tools and techniques available for leadership development. The key is to be open to learning and to adapt the tools based on the specific needs of the leader and the organization.

Techniques and Tools: Tools and Techniques to Improve Leadership Skills.

In the modern era, with a constantly evolving work environment, the skills required of leaders are continually expanding. In addition to traditional skills such as team leadership or making informed decisions, today's leaders must be resilient, empathetic, innovative, and capable of managing diversity and complexity. As a result, there is a growing emphasis on continuous development and training, and several specific tools and techniques have been created for this purpose.

Gamification has proven to be a powerful motivational lever, allowing leaders to practice in simulated situations and confront real problems in a protected context.

Executive Coaching addresses leaders' individual challenges, offering a tailored and focused experience on specific improvement areas, with the goal of achieving authentic and lasting transformation.

Reverse Mentoring acknowledges that learning can come from any level of the organization. The wisdom and experience of seasoned leaders are essential, but the fresh perspectives and digital skills of young professionals are equally valuable.

Leadership Diaries promote self-reflection, a crucial skill in a world where adaptation and self-improvement are essential.

Leadership Networks and Mastermind Groups offer networking opportunities, sharing, and mutual learning. In these networks, leaders can share challenges, triumphs, and lessons learned, expanding their horizons and gaining new perspectives.

Visualization Techniques and Mindfulness Training bring attention to the importance of mental health and well-being, recognizing that a leader must first take care of themselves to take care of others.

Innovation Labs and Immersive Workshops are practical tools that promote innovation and growth. They allow leaders to experiment, prototype, and innovate in a supportive environment.

Finally, Change Management Training is vital in a world where change is the only constant. Leaders must not only manage change but also guide their teams through it, making this type of training essential.

In conclusion, the tools and techniques to improve leadership skills are as diverse as the challenges that today's leaders must face. The key to effective leadership does not lie in mastering a specific tool or technique but in the willingness to learn and adapt continuously, leveraging the wide range of resources available for professional development.

12. Leadership and Innovation: How Leaders Can Foster and Support Innovation.

Innovation is the driving force behind many successful companies in the modern era. In the current context, characterized by rapid technological evolution and a constantly changing market environment, innovation is not only desirable but often necessary for the long-term survival and prosperity of an organization. Leaders play a crucial role in guiding and supporting this innovative spirit.

1. Innovation Culture: Leaders must first create a corporate culture that values and rewards innovation. This may involve embracing risk, tolerating mistakes (viewing them as learning opportunities), and encouraging experimentation. An open culture where ideas can flow freely without fear of criticism is essential for promoting creativity.

2. Organizational Structuring: A flexible and non-hierarchical work environment can facilitate the flow of ideas and reduce bureaucratic obstacles. Some companies implement cross-functional teams or separate innovation units to focus exclusively on new products or solutions.

3. Continuous Training: Providing ongoing training to team members not only enhances existing skills but also introduces new concepts and technologies, fueling an innovative approach to problem-solving.

4. External Collaboration: Collaborating with universities, startups, incubators, or other companies can offer new perspectives and access to expertise and resources that may not be available internally.

5. Adequate Resources: Innovation often requires investments, whether it's time, money, or human resources. Leaders must ensure the necessary resources are allocated for experimenting and developing new ideas.

6. Active Listening: Innovative leaders are excellent listeners. They pay attention to customer needs, market trends, employee feedback, and adjust their strategies accordingly.

7. Lead by Example: Leaders must be the first to demonstrate innovative thinking, experiment with new ideas and approaches, and encourage others to do the same.

8. Recognition and Reward: Recognizing and rewarding innovative ideas and team members' efforts can further incentivize creativity and commitment to innovation.

9. Clear Communication: Leaders must clearly communicate the vision and goals of innovation within the organization, ensuring that everyone is aligned and headed in the same direction.

10. Adaptability: Finally, leaders must be prepared to adapt. Innovation can lead to unexpected changes, and a leader's ability to navigate through these changes while maintaining a focus on the long-term vision is crucial.

In summary, innovation is not a one-time event but rather a continuous process that requires commitment, resources, and an open mindset. Leaders who succeed in integrating innovation into the culture, structure, and daily operations of their organizations are likely to lead their teams to lasting success in the modern market.

Leadership and Innovation: Further Reflections

Long-Term Vision: Effective leaders have the ability to see beyond the immediate horizon. While others focus on daily operations, these leaders can envision how products, services, or markets may look in the future. This long-term vision enables them to anticipate challenges and opportunities, charting a course that positions their organization for an advantage.

Safe Environments for Experimentation: Not every innovative idea will succeed, and successful leaders understand this. They create environments where their teams feel safe to propose new ideas, even if they may fail. Such an environment eliminates the fear of failure and encourages a "trial and learning" mindset, which is crucial for innovation.

Maintaining a Curious Mindset: Curiosity is a distinctive trait of innovative leaders. They are always looking for new approaches, new technologies, and new business models. This relentless pursuit of "what's out there" helps them stay ahead of market changes and bring fresh ideas into the organization.

Network of Connections: Innovative leaders tend to have a wide network of contacts in various industries and sectors. These connections provide a valuable source of inspiration and a different perspective on issues or challenges. Collaborating with people outside their own industry can lead to innovative solutions that might not have been possible otherwise.

Observing and Analyzing Data: In the digital age, data is a goldmine of information. Innovative leaders use tools and technologies to analyze this data and derive insights that can guide strategic decisions. This data-driven approach ensures that innovation is guided not only by intuition but also by concrete evidence.

Balancing Preservation and Renewal: While innovation is crucial, it's equally important to maintain what works. Innovative leaders know when to innovate and when to preserve. They strike a balance between adopting new ideas and maintaining traditions and practices that have worked in the past.

Continuous Feedback: Innovation is not a linear path. It requires ongoing iterations and improvements. Leaders who promote innovation encourage a constant flow of feedback from customers, partners, and team members, using it to refine and enhance new ideas.

The Importance of Organizational Culture in Innovation: One of the primary influencers of an organization's ability to innovate is its culture. If an organization's culture values creativity, learning, and experimentation, innovative ideas are more likely to emerge. Conversely, a culture that punishes mistakes and values conformity and short-term performance can stifle any innovation attempts.

Continuous Training and Learning: Change and innovation go hand in hand. Leaders wishing to promote innovation encourage continuous training and learning. Whether through formal courses, seminars, workshops, or simple brainstorming sessions, these leaders understand the importance of keeping themselves and their teams informed and ready to adapt to new methods and technologies.

Taking a Holistic Approach: While many people associate innovation primarily with new products or technologies, innovative leaders recognize that it can manifest in many ways. It can involve innovating internal processes, business models, marketing strategies, or customer service approaches. Looking at innovation from different angles can lead to unexpected discoveries.

Encouraging Diversity of Thought: Diversity is not just about demographic characteristics like gender, ethnicity, or age. Diversity of thought is essential for innovation. Bringing together people with diverse experiences, backgrounds, and viewpoints can lead to more creative and innovative solutions than homogeneous groups.

Building Strategic Partnerships: In an interconnected world, few companies can afford to operate in silos. Proactive leaders in promoting innovation often seek partnerships and collaborations with other companies, universities, research institutions, or startups. These collaborations can offer new perspectives, expertise, and resources that can accelerate the innovation process.

Dedicated Innovation Resources: While innovation can emerge from any part of an organization, having dedicated resources, such as an innovation team or lab, can help centralize and focus efforts. These entities can explore new ideas without the daily pressures of business operations, allowing them to experiment and test in a more controlled environment.

Actively Listening to the Market: In addition to looking within the organization, innovative leaders keep their ears open to market changes and trends. This can include monitoring competitors, listening to customers, participating in industry fairs, or observing global trends. This sensitivity to external signals allows them to anticipate changes and position themselves proactively.

Maintaining a Balance Between Innovation and Risk: While innovation requires a certain degree of risk, it's important for leaders to find a balance. This means carefully evaluating the potential returns of an innovative idea against the associated risks, ensuring that the organization doesn't stretch too far or expose itself to uncontrolled dangers.

In essence, leadership in innovation is not just about having great ideas but creating an environment where these ideas can flourish, be tested, adapted, and ultimately implemented.

Leadership and Innovation: Conclusion

Innovation is often seen as the engine driving the growth and success of businesses in the contemporary era. However, innovation doesn't simply emerge out of thin air. Behind every successful innovation, there's a leader or leadership team that guides, inspires, and facilitates the process.

1. **Understanding the Importance of Innovation:** Effective leadership recognizes that to remain competitive in a constantly evolving world, companies must be ready to innovate. This doesn't just mean adopting the latest technologies but regularly rethinking strategies, processes, and business models.

2. **Creating an Innovation-Friendly Environment:** This environment promotes experimentation, accepts failure as part of the learning process, and values diverse thinking. A leader must be adept at removing bureaucratic obstacles, providing necessary resources, and encouraging creative thinking.

3. **Maintaining a Holistic Perspective:** Innovative leadership acknowledges that opportunities can emerge from any part of the organization. Innovation isn't just about products or technologies; it can involve processes, customer interactions, or business models.

4. **Listening and Feedback:** The most innovative companies often adopt customer-centric approaches based on actively listening to their needs and adapting offerings accordingly. Leadership, in this context, is responsible for establishing effective feedback channels.

5. **Balancing Risks and Opportunities:** While innovation entails risks, it also offers growth and differentiation opportunities. Leadership must, therefore, strike a balance, understanding when it's time to take bold initiatives and when caution is warranted.

6. **Continuous Training and Growth:** The world is changing rapidly. Companies and

leaders that invest in continuous training and learning are better positioned to lead innovation rather than merely reacting to it.

7. **External Collaboration and Networking:** The most innovative solutions often arise from collaboration. Whether it's partnering with startups, universities, or even competitors, innovation-leading organizations are those that know how to look beyond their own boundaries.

In summary, leadership in innovation requires a combination of vision, strategy, execution, and adaptability. The role of a leader isn't just to drive change but also to inspire and enable others to contribute to the innovation journey. In the modern business world, where change is the only constant, the ability to lead innovation isn't just desirable; it's essential for long-term survival and success.

15.Leadership Training: The Importance of Continuous Development

In a rapidly changing and evolving world, a leader's ability to adapt and develop new skills is crucial. Leadership training is not a one-time, defined process but rather an ongoing journey of growth and development. Let's examine the nature and importance of leadership training:

1. **Adaptability in a Changing World:** The business, technological, and socio-cultural landscape is constantly shifting. Leaders who invest in their training are better prepared to face these challenges and guide their organizations through periods of turbulence.

2. **Refreshing Leadership Skills:** Even leadership skills that were relevant yesterday may not be so today. Continuous training allows leaders to stay updated on the latest trends, theories, and leadership skills.

3. **Emotional Intelligence:** One of the most critical aspects of leadership is the ability to understand and manage one's own emotions and those of others. Leadership training often addresses this aspect, helping leaders develop empathy and self-awareness.

4. **Networking:** Training courses provide opportunities to interact with other leaders and professionals. These interactions can lead to new perspectives, ideas, and even business opportunities.

5. **Complex Problem-Solving:** In an increasingly interconnected world, problems

become more complex. Leadership training can help develop critical and strategic thinking skills.

6. **Ethics and Integrity:** With rising expectations of transparency and corporate ethics from consumers and stakeholders, it's crucial that leaders are trained to make ethical and responsible decisions.

7. **Mentoring and Coaching:** An important component of leadership training is learning how to develop other talents. This can include formal mentoring, coaching, or even creating development programs for future leaders within the organization.

8. **Self-Assessment:** Many training programs encourage self-reflection. This allows leaders to take a moment to assess their strengths, weaknesses, and areas for improvement.

9. **Simulations and Case Studies:** Training often utilizes practical methods like simulations or case studies to help leaders put what they've learned into practice in a controlled environment.

10. **Learning Culture:** Finally, investing in leadership training can help establish a culture of learning within the organization. This can lead to greater openness to change and innovation.

Leadership training goes beyond traditional classrooms or training sessions. In fact, effective leadership training often incorporates a range of methodologies and approaches, ensuring holistic learning.

Experiential Training: This is a form of training where participants learn through hands-on experiences rather than pure theory. It may include activities like role-playing, simulations, or team-building exercises. This type of training helps leaders internalize what they've learned, putting their knowledge into practice in real-world situations.

360-Degree Feedback: This is a method where leaders receive feedback from various team members, superiors, and peers. This comprehensive overview provides a clear picture of strengths and areas for improvement and can be a valuable tool for personal growth.

Peer-to-Peer Learning: Learning doesn't only happen through an instructor or coach but also through interaction with peers. Sharing experiences and challenges with peers can offer valuable insights and new perspectives.

Online and Technological Training: With the advent of technology, leadership training is no longer limited to classrooms. Webinars, online courses, e-learning platforms, and mobile apps have opened up new avenues for training, allowing for flexible and personalized learning.

Cross-Functional Training: Leadership is not just about managing people; it's also about understanding various functions within an organization. Cross-functional training exposes leaders to different departments and roles, helping them better understand the challenges and opportunities in each area.

Study Tours and Field Visits: Visits to other organizations or even trips abroad to study best practices can provide leaders with valuable external perspectives and innovative ideas to bring back to their organization.

Reflective Thinking and Journaling: A fundamental part of training is reflection. Many programs encourage leaders to keep a journal where they can reflect on their experiences, challenges, and what they have learned.

Coaching and Mentoring Methodologies: While coaching often focuses on specific goals and developing particular skills, mentoring revolves around a long-term relationship, with a mentor offering wisdom, experience, and advice.

Cultural Training: In a globalized world, understanding diverse cultures and norms is crucial. Cultural training prepares leaders to interact effectively with teams, customers, and partners from different cultural backgrounds.

In summary, it's clear that leadership training is a vast and multifaceted field. It goes beyond traditional classroom sessions or seminars and embraces a wide range of methodologies and approaches. While the methods may vary, the goal remains the same: to develop capable, empathetic, and visionary leaders ready to tackle the challenges of the 21st century.

Leadership training is deeply intertwined with the fabric of continuous learning. In a rapidly evolving business environment, leaders can no longer afford to rest on their laurels. This is why several new trends and practices in leadership training have emerged, reflecting the need to adapt and grow in an ever-changing world.

Adaptability and Agile Learning: In an era marked by rapid and often unexpected changes, a leader's ability to adapt has become crucial. Training now emphasizes the importance of developing an agile mindset—one that not only accepts change but actively welcomes it as an opportunity.

Emotional Intelligence: The ability to recognize, understand, and manage one's own emotions, as well as those of others, has become a key competency. Training programs now integrate emotional intelligence as a central pillar, recognizing that technical skills alone are insufficient for effective leadership.

Distributed Leadership: Leadership training no longer exclusively targets those at the top. There is a growing awareness that leadership can emerge from any level within an organization. This distributed approach encourages all team members to take initiative and assume responsibility.

Microlearning: Instead of extended training sessions, microlearning offers small bursts of content that can be consumed in short intervals. This aligns with the fast-paced work environment where leaders may not have the time for full-day training.

Simulations and Virtual Reality: The advent of technology has led to the growth of simulations and virtual reality as training tools. These platforms offer an immersive environment where leaders can confront hypothetical yet realistic scenarios and receive immediate feedback on their decisions.

Peer Learning and Mastermind Groups: Mastermind groups, composed of leaders from diverse organizations, regularly gather to share challenges, solutions, and best practices. Peer sharing offers a different perspective from traditional top-down training.

Wellness Focus: Mental health and overall well-being have become central aspects of leadership training. This reflects the growing awareness that effective leaders must also be balanced and centered individuals.

Values-Based Training: Rather than solely focusing on skills and techniques, many programs now frame leadership training in terms of core values. This helps ensure that leaders are not only competent but also ethical and aligned with the organization's values.

Each element above highlights how leadership training is evolving to reflect the needs of an ever-changing world. Once viewed as an "extra" or a "bonus," training is now considered an absolute necessity, a continuous investment in the future of the organization and its leaders.

Leadership training has undergone a radical transformation in recent decades, adapting to the challenges and opportunities of a globalized and technologically advanced business environment. Its essence is no longer limited to acquiring managerial skills but rather to shaping a holistic individual capable of successfully navigating complex interpersonal, cultural, and technological dynamics.

One of the most important realizations in this field is the recognition that leadership is not a rigid or static quality but rather a dynamic set of skills, attitudes, and values that can and should be continuously refined. This has led to a greater emphasis on personal and professional growth, not just as leaders but as individuals. The concept of "leaders as learners" is now central in many training programs, suggesting that, no matter how much experience or knowledge one may have, there is always room to learn and grow.

Incorporating emotional intelligence into leadership training highlights an acknowledgment of the complexity of human nature. A leader is not only a decision-maker or strategist but also a communicator, mediator, and mentor. The ability to understand and manage one's own emotions and those of others has become as crucial as processing information and making informed decisions.

Technology has also played a pivotal role in the transformation of leadership training. Tools like virtual reality, simulations, and microlearning not only make learning more accessible but also more practical and contextualized. Leaders can now "experience" hypothetical yet realistic scenarios, make real-time decisions, and see the consequences of those decisions, all in a controlled environment.

Lastly, the idea that leadership can and should be ethical and values-based is now at the heart of training. In an increasingly interconnected world, leaders are not only accountable to their immediate stakeholders but also to a global community. Leadership training, therefore, is not just about acquiring skills but also about cultivating a moral compass.

In conclusion, leadership training in the 21st century is an ongoing journey of self-discovery, learning, and adaptation. It is not a destination to reach but rather an ever-evolving path, fueled by insatiable curiosity and a deep commitment to service and excellence. It prepares leaders not only to address the challenges of the present but also to anticipate and shape the future.

Case Studies: Real Examples of Leadership in Action, Successes, and Failures

Case studies are a fundamental element for concretely understanding how leadership theories and principles manifest in reality. Observing real examples of leadership in action, both in terms of successes and failures, allows for valuable lessons to be learned and offers a clearer and more tangible insight into the challenges and opportunities that leaders may encounter.

Steve Jobs and Apple: Steve Jobs' story is often cited as an emblematic example of visionary leadership. Jobs was not only an innovator but also knew how to motivate and inspire his teams. However, he was not immune to criticism, often perceived as demanding and difficult. His ability to recognize his own mistakes, such as initially excluding third-party applications on the iPhone, and to quickly rectify them, was one of his greatest strengths.

Satya Nadella and Microsoft: After taking the reins from Steve Ballmer, Nadella initiated a cultural transformation within Microsoft, shifting the focus from mere competition to achieving a greater goal. He also recognized the importance of cloud computing, leading Microsoft in that direction and resulting in a revival of the company.

Indra Nooyi and PepsiCo: During her tenure as CEO of PepsiCo, Nooyi aimed to balance shareholder expectations with a long-term vision for the company. She introduced healthier products and emphasized the importance of sustainability.

Blockbuster vs. Netflix: While Netflix embraced the future with its online subscription model, Blockbuster lagged in adapting to changes in how people consumed media. This delay in innovation and strategic vision led to Blockbuster's decline.

Theranos and Elizabeth Holmes: A cautionary tale of leadership, the Theranos case shows what can go wrong when transparency and integrity are set aside. While Holmes had a revolutionary vision for blood testing, allegations of fraud and false claims ultimately led to the downfall of the company.

Mary Barra and General Motors: Becoming CEO of GM amid a large-scale recall crisis, Barra faced the challenges head-on, taking responsibility, ensuring transparency, and implementing significant changes within the company to prevent future issues.

Analyzing these and other case studies provides an in-depth understanding of the real dynamics of leadership. Through successes, one can identify the strategies and behaviors that lead to positive outcomes. Similarly, through failures, the importance of foresight, adaptability, and integrity in leadership can be understood.

By examining further examples in the history of business and beyond, it becomes evident how certain decisions, attitudes, and behaviors of leaders have profoundly influenced the fate of their organizations and, in some cases, entire industries or communities.

7. Chesley "Sully" Sullenberger and the Hudson River Landing: This event pertains not to leadership within an organization but rather leadership in a crisis situation. Captain Sullenberger, the pilot of Airbus A320, made the courageous and timely decision to land on the Hudson River after both engines were damaged by a bird strike. His calmness and decision-making ability saved the lives of everyone on board.

8. Jeff Bezos and Amazon: Starting as a modest online bookstore, Bezos transformed Amazon into one of the global giants of e-commerce and technology. His mantra of "Day 1," emphasizing the importance of maintaining a startup mentality even in a large organization, guided the company through continuous innovations.

9. Howard Schultz and Starbucks: Schultz turned Starbucks from a small coffee chain in Seattle into one of the world's largest chains. His vision was not limited to selling coffee but rather creating a "third place" between home and work where people could relax and socialize. However, Schultz also faced criticisms, such as those related to sustainability and worker conditions.

10. Nokia and the Smartphone Industry: Once a leader in the mobile phone market, Nokia lost its dominant position due to a series of strategic errors and a lack of innovative vision. While Apple and Android made their way into the smartphone market, Nokia lagged behind, illustrating how inadequate or reactive leadership can lead to the decline of an entire company.

11. Jack Ma and Alibaba: Starting from a small apartment in China, Jack Ma founded Alibaba, which became one of the world's largest e-commerce platforms. But he didn't stop at e-commerce; with vision and determination, he expanded Alibaba into areas like finance, entertainment, and cloud computing.

12. Kodak and Digital Photography: Kodak, once a leader in the photography industry, underestimated the impact of digital photography, despite having the expertise to become a pioneer in that field. Resistance to change and a lack of proactive vision led to the company's decline.

Every leader and every company has its peculiarities, but what emerges from these case studies is that leadership requires vision, adaptability, courage, and integrity. The decisions made by leaders can have enormous repercussions, both positive and negative, on the people and organizations they lead. It is essential for future leaders to study these examples to draw valuable lessons and insights.

13. Theranos and Elizabeth Holmes: This biotechnology startup promised to revolutionize laboratory testing with a simple drop of blood. Led by the young and charismatic Elizabeth Holmes, Theranos raised billions of dollars from investors. However, claims about the effectiveness of its technology were greatly exaggerated. The Theranos case serves as a warning about the importance of transparency and integrity, as well as the dangers of a corporate culture that does not tolerate critical voices.

14. Satya Nadella and Microsoft: When Nadella took the helm of Microsoft, the company was seen as declining, overshadowed by competitors like Apple and Google. However, under his leadership, Microsoft experienced a resurgence, focusing on cloud computing and openness to external platforms. Nadella also worked to change the corporate culture, promoting growth and learning rather than internal competition.

15. Blockbuster and Netflix: While Netflix started as a DVD rental service by mail, its ability to adapt and innovate transformed the company into a streaming giant. In contrast, Blockbuster was unable to adapt quickly to changes in consumer behavior and new technologies, leading to its decline. This story illustrates the importance of innovation and vision in staying relevant in an evolving market.

16. Indra Nooyi and PepsiCo: During her tenure as CEO of PepsiCo, Nooyi sought to balance the company's growth with sustainability and responsibility. She introduced healthier products, reduced the amount of sugar and salt in existing products, and focused on sustainability initiatives. Her leadership showed how a company can be both profitable and socially responsible.

17. Lehman Brothers and the 2008 Financial Crisis: The bankruptcy of Lehman Brothers in 2008 was one of the largest in history and played a key role in triggering the global financial crisis. Lehman's inability to manage risks properly and its corporate culture based on excessive risk-taking led to its collapse. This event highlighted the importance of corporate governance, risk management, and ethics in leadership.

18. Mellody Hobson and Diversity: As co-CEO of Ariel Investments, Hobson has been a passionate advocate for diversity on boards of directors and in executive positions. She has openly spoken about the benefits of increased diversity and inclusion, highlighting how diverse perspectives can lead to better business decisions.

Each case study presents unique lessons and points for reflection. The actions and decisions of leaders can have a profound impact, influencing not only the fate of their organizations but also the global economy, society, and individuals. In many of these examples, it can be seen how the ability to see beyond the horizon, adapt to change, and remain true to ethical principles has been crucial to success or failure.

The complex and multifaceted nature of leadership is highlighted when we delve deeply into various case studies. These not only reveal the decisions and actions of leaders but also the environment in which they operate and how they react to challenges. From the dramatic fall of Theranos, which underscores the importance of transparency and integrity, to the resurgence of Microsoft under Satya Nadella, we see how a leader's ability to innovate and adapt can make the difference between an organization's success and failure.

Blockbuster and Netflix, with their intertwined stories, offer a clear lesson on the importance of recognizing changes in consumer behavior and adapting quickly to new market trends. Meanwhile, Indra Nooyi's journey with PepsiCo demonstrates how a leader can guide a company toward sustainability and social responsibility while ensuring growth and profitability.

The bankruptcy of Lehman Brothers and the ensuing financial crisis illustrate how leadership choices can have global repercussions, highlighting the importance of strong corporate governance and risk management. Mellody Hobson, through her work and opinions, shows that diversity and inclusion are not just moral issues but essential for the growth and success of organizations.

These case studies, with their various challenges and outcomes, emphasize some fundamental themes:

1. Adaptability: In an ever-changing world, a leader's ability to adapt to change is crucial.

2. Long-Term Vision: In addition to addressing immediate concerns, leaders must have a clear vision of the future and work to realize it.

3. Integrity and Ethics: Truthfulness, honesty, and adherence to moral principles are non-negotiable. Leaders must lead with integrity, creating a culture that values ethics.

4. Listening and Inclusion: An effective leader listens to diverse voices within and outside the organization, encouraging an inclusive environment.

5. Risk Management: Recognizing, assessing, and managing risks is crucial, especially in an unpredictable environment.**

In conclusion, leadership is not based on a fixed formula or a set of rigid rules. It is a combination of innate characteristics, acquired skills, lived experiences, and decisions made. Each case study offers a lens through which we can examine the complexities of leadership, learning valuable lessons about what works, what doesn't, and how we can aspire to become better leaders in our own domains.

15. Digital Leadership: The importance of leadership in the digital age and how to navigate digital transformation.

Digital Leadership: The importance of leadership in the digital age and how to navigate digital transformation.

Digital leadership has emerged as a critical component in the modern era, where technology and digitization are rapidly transforming organizations and societies worldwide. It goes beyond mere understanding of technologies; it's about how to lead organizations in an era where digital permeates every aspect of business and operations.

Understanding the Digital Landscape: Digital transformation is not just a matter of adopting new tools or technologies; it's a radical reconfiguration of how businesses operate and deliver value to their customers. The digital era has led to the creation of new business models, altering the dynamics between companies and customers, and introducing new challenges and opportunities. This context requires leaders who deeply understand the impact of digitization on their industry and can successfully navigate through this new landscape.

Wide Range of Required Skills: A digital leader must possess a combination of technical skills and soft skills. These include an understanding of emerging technologies like artificial intelligence, machine learning, and blockchain, and how they can be applied to create value. At the same time, they must have skills such as strategic vision, change management, effective communication, and the ability to inspire and motivate teams amidst uncertainty.

Culture of Innovation: To thrive in the digital age, organizations must embrace a culture of innovation. Digital leaders promote environments where failure is seen as a learning opportunity, where experimentation is encouraged, and where teams are empowered to make data-driven decisions.

Data-Driven Mindset: In the digital era, leaders must have a data-driven mindset. This means not only having access to data but also knowing how to interpret it and use it to make informed decisions, predict trends, and personalize offerings for customers.

Cybersecurity and Ethics: Digitalization has brought new security and privacy threats. Digital leaders must ensure that their organizations adopt best practices in cybersecurity. In addition to security, there is a growing need to consider ethics, especially when it comes to technologies like AI, ensuring that decisions are made responsibly and with consideration for the human impact.

Collaboration and Networking: Leadership in the digital era also requires strong collaboration skills. As technology and digitalization often eliminate traditional silos within organizations, leaders must be able to work cross-functionally, connecting with different functions, business units, and even other organizations or industries.

Digital leadership goes beyond just having knowledge of technological tools; it embraces a mindset that integrates the digital into all facets of business management. Every decision, every strategy, every interaction with employees or customers is influenced by the digital context. In such a connected world, a leader's ability to navigate this digital environment becomes crucial.

Importance of Flexibility and Adaptability: In a rapidly changing environment like the digital one, strategies and solutions that work today may not be effective tomorrow. Leaders must, therefore, develop a high degree of flexibility, being ready to adapt to new challenges and opportunities as they arise. The ability to learn and unlearn quickly becomes essential, as new tools and platforms are continually introduced into the digital landscape.

Human Connection in the Digital Age: Although technology plays a predominant role, digital leadership must not overlook the importance of human relationships. Even in a technology-dominated context, a leader's ability to connect, understand, and motivate people remains at the core of their success. This implies the importance of balancing digital interactions with face-to-face ones and using technology to enhance, rather than replace, human connections.

Lateral Thinking and Creativity: With the vast amount of data and tools available, digital leaders have the opportunity to experiment with new approaches and solutions. This requires an open mindset, ready to challenge the status quo and think outside the box. Creativity becomes a valuable attribute, allowing leaders to see opportunities where others see obstacles.

Holistic Vision: Digitalization has made organizations more interconnected than ever. Therefore, leaders can no longer afford to view their decisions in silos. A decision made in one area can have repercussions throughout the organization. Leaders must, therefore, adopt a holistic vision, considering the cascading effect of their decisions and ensuring they align with the overall strategy of the organization.

Continuous Education: Finally, the digital age requires a constant commitment to learning. This includes not only keeping up with new technologies but also understanding how these technologies influence human behavior, market dynamics, and business strategy. Courses, seminars, conferences, and other learning opportunities should become a regular part of a leader's agenda.

By incorporating these considerations into their daily practice, leaders can ensure they are effectively equipped to guide their organizations in an era dominated by digitalization. It's not just about adopting technology but meaningfully integrating it into every aspect of leadership.

Within the realm of digital leadership, it's crucial to recognize that digital transformation goes beyond the adoption of new technologies; it also involves the transformation of organizational culture and structures. This transformation entails a deep understanding of how digital technologies are reshaping the competitive landscape and customer expectations, and therefore, how organizations must evolve.

Specific Digital Skills: Today's leaders must have a thorough understanding of emerging technologies such as artificial intelligence, blockchain, virtual and augmented reality, and the Internet of Things (IoT). This doesn't necessarily mean becoming experts in these areas but rather having a solid understanding of how these technologies can be applied to create value and how they might impact the business.

Data-Driven Mentality: In the digital era, decisions must be informed by data. Leaders should be comfortable working with large amounts of data, interpreting it, and using it to make informed decisions. This also involves an understanding of potential pitfalls, such as misleading or distorted data.

Cybersecurity: With the rise of digital threats, cybersecurity has become a crucial concern. Leaders must be aware of the risks associated with digitalization and take appropriate measures to protect the organization's information and resources.

Customer-Centric Approach: Digitalization has empowered customers like never before. They have access to a vast amount of information and can compare products and services with a simple click. Leaders must recognize this dynamic and continuously strive to enhance the customer experience through digital solutions.

Organizational Agility: In response to the rapidly evolving digital environment, organizations need to become more agile. Leaders must foster an environment where change can be implemented quickly, where teams can form and reform in response to new opportunities or challenges, and where innovation is encouraged and rewarded.

Collaboration and Communication: Leadership in the digital age also requires a greater emphasis on collaboration. With the increasing complexity of projects and the integration of various technologies, collaboration between teams and departments is essential. Effective communication, both within and outside the organization, becomes a fundamental skill.

Growth Mindset: The digital environment is constantly evolving, and leaders must adopt a growth mindset, ready to evolve and adapt. This involves a willingness for continuous learning, experimentation, and the ability to accept and learn from failures.

These are just some facets of leadership in the digital era. Over time, the importance of digital leadership will continue to grow, and successful leaders will be those who recognize and embrace the opportunities and challenges of this new era.

Digital leadership represents a fundamental evolution of traditional leadership principles in response to the technological and digital revolutions shaping our world. The digital era is not just about adopting new technologies but rather a restructuring of the mental approach, organizational culture, and operational methods within businesses and institutions.

Strategic and Holistic Vision: Digital leaders have the responsibility not only to understand individual emerging technologies but also to see how they converge and interact to create new opportunities and challenges. The ability to have a holistic view, to understand how, for example, AI, augmented reality, blockchain, and IoT can converge to create new solutions, is crucial. This vision must be accompanied by the ability to translate these insights into tangible operational strategies.

Digital Ethics and Responsibility: With great power comes great responsibility. In the digital era, issues of privacy, data security, and cybersecurity are in the spotlight. Leaders must ensure that their organizations not only comply with laws and regulations but also operate with integrity and ethics. They should be the foremost advocates for the rights of their customers and stakeholders and ensure that technology is used ethically and responsibly.

Training and Development: Continuous training is essential in the digital era. As new technologies continue to emerge at an unprecedented pace, leaders must ensure that both themselves and their teams are constantly updated and trained. This means not only technical training but also developing a mindset of adaptability and continuous learning.

Measuring Success and KPIs: Digital leadership also requires a reevaluation of how success is measured. While traditional performance indicators may still be relevant, leaders must also consider new KPIs related to digital adoption, online engagement, the effectiveness of digital platforms, and other related aspects.

Conclusion: In summary, digital leadership is not just about adopting new technologies but represents a profound transformation in how leaders think, act, and guide their organizations in the digital era. This transformation requires a combination of technical skills, strategic capabilities, and a strong ethical sense. In a world where technology continues to evolve at a dizzying pace, successful leaders will be those who can confidently navigate this ever-changing landscape while keeping people and values at the forefront. Leadership in the digital era is as much a matter of the mind and heart as it is of technical competence.

16. Leadership and Mental Health: Managing Stress, Burnout, and Self-Care for Leaders.

Leadership, while a position that offers power and authority, carries a high level of responsibility, expectations, and pressure. These factors can significantly impact the mental health of leaders. Managing stress, preventing burnout, and self-care are essential elements for maintaining a leader's effectiveness and well-being.

Stress and Leadership: Stress is a natural response to life's challenges and pressures. However, leaders often face higher levels of stress due to the expectations and responsibilities that come with their position. Tough decisions, internal conflicts, external pressures, performance expectations, and the continuous need for innovation can accumulate, leading to unsustainable levels of stress.

Burnout: Burnout is a professional exhaustion syndrome that can result from unmanaged chronic work-related stress. It manifests through feelings of energy depletion, cynicism or detachment from one's work, and a sense of reduced professional efficacy. For leaders, burnout can have devastating effects, not only on their mental health but also on their ability to lead effectively.

Self-Care Strategies: To prevent stress and burnout, leaders must implement self-care strategies. These can include:

1. **Breaks and Reflection:** Taking time to disconnect, reflect, and recharge is essential. This can involve taking short breaks during the day, scheduling vacations, or simply dedicating time to hobbies and interests outside of work.

2. **Exercise and Nutrition:** Maintaining a healthy physique has a direct impact on mental health. Regular exercise can help reduce stress, improve mood, and boost energy.

3. **Social Connections:** Maintaining close bonds with friends, family, and colleagues can provide an essential support network.

4. **Mindfulness and Meditation:** These practices can help center the mind, reduce anxiety, and improve concentration.

5. **Training and Therapy:** Having a therapist or coach can provide a safe space to explore challenges and feelings while offering strategies and tools to manage stress.

Recognizing Signs: It is crucial for leaders to recognize signs of stress and burnout in themselves and their team members. This can include changes in behavior, social withdrawal, decreased performance, or expressions of despair.

The Role of the Work Environment: The work environment can significantly impact the mental health of leaders. A toxic environment characterized by gossip, office politics, or lack of support can amplify feelings of isolation or dissatisfaction. In contrast, a positive work environment can act as a buffer against stress and provide an essential support network.

Unrealistic Expectations: In many business contexts, there's an unspoken expectation that leaders should always be strong, unstoppable, and infallible. This myth of the "superman" or "superwoman" leader can prevent leaders from seeking help when needed, exacerbating feelings of isolation or incompetence.

Technology and Constant Connectivity: In the era of digitization, leaders are often presumed to be available 24/7, 365 days a year. This constant connectivity can erode the boundaries between work and personal life, making it difficult for leaders to disconnect and recover.

Stigmatization of Mental Health: Despite progress in understanding mental health, there is still some stigma surrounding the topic, especially in business settings. Leaders may hesitate to discuss their mental health challenges or seek help for fear of being seen as weak or incapable.

The Value of Feedback: Receiving constructive feedback can help leaders assess and address their areas for improvement. However, many leaders do not receive honest feedback due to their position. This lack can lead to doubts and uncertainties, further fueling stress.

Coping and Prevention Strategies: Many leaders have developed personal strategies to manage stress and prevent burnout. These can include relaxation techniques like deep breathing, the use of mindfulness apps, or practices like yoga. Some leaders may also benefit from creating support networks with other leaders, where they can share challenges and solutions in a safe and supportive environment.

External Resources: Beyond personal strategies, there are many external resources available to leaders. These can include specialized mental health consultants for professionals, employee assistance programs, or seminars and workshops focused on resilience and stress management.

In Conclusion: In conclusion, while the position of a leader can be extremely rewarding, it also brings unique challenges in terms of mental health. Recognizing and addressing these challenges is essential for the longevity and effectiveness of any leader.

Leadership, as a crucial function in guiding teams, organizations, or entire nations, is intrinsically linked to significant responsibilities and expectations. The importance of addressing mental health issues for leaders is, therefore, a fundamental component to ensure not only their personal well-being but also the health and productivity of the entire organization.

The very nature of leadership implies the need to make often complex decisions, manage interpersonal relationships, and deal with conflicts, which can be significant sources of stress. The constant pressure, resulting from balancing the needs of various stakeholders, can lead to feelings of isolation, exhaustion, and, in some cases, more severe disorders such as depression.

The contemporary work context, characterized by rapid technological advancements and expectations of immediate responsiveness, has further increased the stress load on leaders. The possibility of always being connected and available has blurred the boundaries between work and leisure time, making it even more challenging for leaders to find moments of rest and reflection.

Unfortunately, despite growing awareness of the importance of mental health, there is still some reluctance to openly discuss these issues, especially in business contexts. Leaders may hesitate to share or address their mental health challenges for fear of being perceived as vulnerable or less capable. This taboo can further exacerbate the problem, preventing those in need from seeking help.

However, there is a growing understanding of the importance of providing leaders with the necessary resources and tools to manage and prevent mental health issues. This can include stress management training, well-being support programs, and encouraging an open and inclusive corporate culture where mental health is not stigmatized but rather viewed as a fundamental component of overall well-being.

In conclusion, addressing challenges related to mental health in leadership is not just a matter of individual well-being. It is a strategic necessity to ensure that leaders can lead effectively, with empathy and clarity. By ensuring that leaders have the resources and support to manage their mental health challenges, the entire organization is positioned for sustainable success and long-term well-being.

17. Teams and Leadership: Creating, Leading, and Sustaining High-Performance Teams.

The role of a leader in creating, leading, and sustaining high-performance teams is of crucial importance. Teams are often at the heart of organizations, whether they are small startups or large multinational corporations. A high-performance team can lead to exceptional results, while a dysfunctional team can cause delays, costs, and tensions. Here are some detailed considerations on the subject:

1. Team Formation: The first step in forming a high-performance team is selecting its members. This involves not only choosing individuals with the right technical skills but also with the right behavioral characteristics and the ability to work well together. Diversity within teams, both in terms of skills and life experiences, can provide a variety of perspectives and approaches that enrich decision-making and creativity.

2. Setting Clear Goals: Once the team is formed, it is essential to establish a clear vision and concrete goals. These should be SMART (Specific, Measurable, Achievable, Relevant, Time-bound) and shared by all team members.

3. Providing Resources and Training: High-performance teams need the right resources and training to excel in their work. This can include cutting-edge technologies, ongoing training opportunities, and access to experts or mentors.

4. Building a Trusting Environment: Trust is the foundation of every successful team. Members must feel free to express their opinions, ask questions, and share concerns without fear of repercussions. Transparency, openness, and clear communication by the leader are crucial for building this trust.

5. Conflict Management: Even in the best teams, conflicts can arise. A good leader recognizes signs of tension and intervenes to resolve issues before they escalate. This may require active listening, mediation, and sometimes, difficult decisions for the sake of the team and the project.

6. Recognition and Rewards: High-performance teams are often highly motivated. Recognizing their efforts and rewarding success can further enhance this motivation. This doesn't just mean bonuses or promotions but also praise, professional development opportunities, and other non-monetary incentives.

7. Review and Adaptation: High-performance teams are not static. They grow, evolve, and adapt to new challenges. Leaders must be ready to periodically review the team's structure, dynamics, and goals and make the necessary adjustments to keep it at the forefront.

In conclusion, leading a high-performance team requires a combination of technical, interpersonal, and leadership skills. An effective leader recognizes the potential of each team member, provides the necessary resources and support, and creates an environment in which everyone can thrive. The ultimate goal is a cohesive team that overcomes challenges and produces exceptional results.

The Relationship Between a Leader and Their Team: The relationship between a leader and their team is fundamental to the success of any initiative. While we have already touched on fundamental aspects such as training, trust, and conflict management, there are many other elements that can influence a team's effectiveness.

Continuous Feedback: Feedback is the key to improvement and ensuring that the team is moving in the right direction. An effective leader provides feedback not only in formal moments such as performance reviews but consistently. This feedback can be positive, recognizing and rewarding good performance, or constructive, helping team members understand where they can improve and how to do so.

Two-Way Communication: While it is essential for a leader to communicate expectations and goals clearly, it is equally important to listen. Two-way communication allows team members to share ideas, concerns, and feedback on decisions. This type of open communication can lead to innovative solutions and ensure that everyone is on the same page.

Empowerment: An effective leader does not micromanage. Instead, they empower their team members, allowing them to make decisions, solve problems, and manage their responsibilities. This not only improves efficiency but also increases team members' confidence and satisfaction.

Team Building: In addition to daily work, it is important for leaders to organize team-building activities. These can range from simple team-building exercises to team retreats. These activities strengthen the bonds among team members, improve communication, and can also increase productivity.

Leadership Development Within the Team:
Visionary leaders recognize the importance of developing future leaders within their team. This can be done through training, mentorship, and providing leadership opportunities at lower levels. Developing future leaders ensures the sustainability and growth of the organization in the long term.

Use of Technology: In the modern era, technology plays a crucial role in team management, especially with the rise of remote work and geographically distributed teams. Using collaboration tools, communication platforms, and project management software can enhance efficiency and keep the team synchronized.

Assessing Team Dynamics: From time to time, it is crucial to take a step back and assess team dynamics. This may include analyzing the team's strengths and weaknesses, identifying areas for improvement, and recognizing where the team excels.

Every team is unique, with its combination of skills, personalities, and dynamics. An effective leader recognizes these singularities and actively works to guide their team to success, ensuring that each team member feels valued, heard, and motivated.

Interpersonal Dynamics in a Team:

Interpersonal dynamics within a team are a central aspect in determining its efficiency and productivity. A leader's ability to understand and influence these dynamics can have a significant impact on the overall performance of the group.

Diversity and Inclusion:

Modern teams are becoming increasingly diverse in terms of gender, age, cultural background, and life experiences. This diversity can lead to a wide range of perspectives that, if managed correctly, can result in more creative and innovative solutions. However, it can also lead to potential tensions or misunderstandings. A leader's ability to create an environment where everyone feels included and valued is crucial to harnessing the benefits of diversity.

Adaptability:

The business world is constantly evolving, and teams must be able to adapt quickly to changes. Whether it's ncw tcchnologies, processes, or markets, a leader must guide their team through these transitions, ensuring that everyone is trained and ready to face new challenges.

Conflict Management:

Conflicts are inevitable in any group. However, if managed correctly, they can become opportunities for growth rather than obstacles. A leader must be able to identify signs of emerging tensions and proactively address them by mediating between conflicting parties and finding solutions that are in the best interest of the team.

Trust and Transparency:

Trust is the foundation of any effective working relationship. To build this trust, a leader must be transparent in their decisions and actions. This means communicating the reasons behind a decision clearly, being open to feedback, and demonstrating consistency between words and actions.

Focus on Team Well-being:

In addition to work pressures, team members may face personal challenges that can affect their well-being and performance. An empathetic leader recognizes the importance of their members' well-being and provides support, which can range from regular breaks to flexible working hours to psychological support programs.

Mentorship and Personal Growth:

A leader focuses not only on short-term results but also looks to the future. This means investing in the growth and development of team members by offering mentorship opportunities, training courses, and constructive feedback.

Resource Management:

Each team member has a unique set of skills and talents. An effective leader recognizes these individual abilities and aligns them with the project's or organization's needs. This not only ensures that the team works efficiently but also ensures that each individual feels valued and motivated.

In summary, team leadership goes beyond managing day-to-day tasks. It's about creating an environment where each member can thrive, bringing value to the organization, and growing both professionally and personally.

Leadership of Effective Teams:

Leading teams, especially high-performance ones, is one of the most demanded and challenging skills in the contemporary professional landscape. The complexity of this task lies not simply in managing a group of individuals but in being able to create, develop, and maintain a collaborative and synergistic environment that maximizes the potential of each member.

Creating Effective Teams:

The first challenge for a leader is the selection and assembly of individuals into a team. Each member should be chosen not only for their technical skills but also for their ability to collaborate, communicate, and integrate into the team's culture. It is essential for a leader to understand and value the diversity of skills, experiences, and perspectives, ensuring a balance between technical skills and soft skills.

Team Development and Growth:

Once the team is formed, the real challenge becomes its continuous development. This includes regular training, mentoring, creating opportunities for mutual feedback, and promoting a culture of continuous learning. The leader should also be attentive to recognizing and celebrating successes while simultaneously addressing and learning from failures.

Maintaining a Positive Environment:

The well-being and morale of the team are fundamental to its performance. This requires open and honest communication, timely conflict resolution, and the promotion of work-life balance. A leader should also be able to identify and intervene in case of burnout or other mental health issues that could affect team members.

Defining Vision and Objectives:

A team needs clear direction. This requires the leader to establish a shared vision and clear objectives, ensuring that each team member understands their role and expectations. This vision should be revisited and adapted regularly based on feedback and changes in the external environment.

Assessment and Feedback:

Finally, to ensure the long-term sustainability and effectiveness of the team, the leader must establish a regular assessment system. This includes collecting feedback from and for each team member, analyzing results against objectives, and adapting leadership strategies based on emerging team needs.

In conclusion, leading high-performance teams goes beyond mere supervision of daily activities. It is an ongoing responsibility of development, support, and innovation, always with the goal of enabling each team member to contribute to the best of their abilities and advance the entire group towards increasingly ambitious goals.

18. Vision and Mission: The Importance of Having a Clear Vision and Mission to Guide Actions and Decisions.

Vision and Mission: The Importance of Having a Clear Vision and Mission to Guide Actions and Decisions.

Vision and mission are essential elements in defining the identity and direction of an organization, a team, or a project. These components help establish a conceptual framework within which decisions are made, strategies are formulated, and resources are allocated. Their importance in the leadership and management landscape cannot be underestimated.

The Vision:

Vision represents a future perspective, an ideal image of what an organization or an individual hopes to achieve over time. It's the horizon toward which one aims, a representation of the ultimate goal. Vision serves as a beacon, illuminating the direction in which an entity desires to move. It can inspire, motivate, and galvanize people toward a common objective. Furthermore, it provides a framework within which successes can be measured and celebrated. An effective vision is ambitious yet achievable and is formulated in clear and motivating terms.

The Mission:

While vision looks to the future, mission focuses on the present, outlining the fundamental purpose of the organization or individual. It describes what the entity does, for whom it does it, and often how it does it. The mission provides a clear definition of the organization's role and value in the broader context, guiding daily activities and strategic decisions. An effective mission is clear, concise, and unambiguous, facilitating understanding and adherence by all involved stakeholders.

Interconnection between Vision and Mission:

Vision and mission are deeply interconnected. Vision provides the destination, while mission defines the path to reach it. Together, these components ensure that an organization maintains a consistent direction and that operational decisions are always aligned with the long-term goal.

Importance for Leaders:

For leaders, establishing a clear vision and mission is crucial for several reasons:

1. **Organizational Alignment:** Clear vision and mission ensure that everyone in the organization is aligned toward the same objectives.

2. **Motivation:** They provide a sense of purpose, inspiring and motivating team members to give their best.

3. **Decision Guidance:** They offer a reference framework that facilitates decision-making, especially in complex or ambiguous situations.

4. **Differentiation:** They help distinguish an organization from others in the market, defining clearly what makes it unique.

Vision and mission are as essential as they are complex. Beyond the basic definition, these statements have deep roots in organizational psychology, corporate culture, and branding strategy.

The Psychological Role:

Vision and mission have a profound impact on the psyche of organization members. They create a sense of belonging and identity. When an individual can relate to a vision or a mission, their dedication and commitment to the organization tend to increase. This psychological connection can positively influence productivity, job satisfaction, and employee retention.

Corporate Culture:

A company's culture is often a reflection of its vision and mission statements. For example, a company with a vision centered on innovation may have a corporate culture that encourages creative thinking and experimentation. Conversely, an organization with a mission focused on tradition and continuity may have a more conservative culture. Leaders must be aware of how vision and mission influence culture and, in turn, how culture can support or hinder the realization of that vision and mission.

Branding Strategy:

In the modern era of marketing, a company's vision and mission are often at the core of its branding strategies. These statements help define the brand's personality, what it represents, and what it promises to its customers. For example, if a company has a mission centered on environmental sustainability, it might use it to position itself as a leader in the green market, attract environmentally conscious customers, and establish partnerships with other sustainability-oriented organizations.

Adaptability and Growth:

Vision and mission statements are not static. As the world changes and businesses grow, these statements can and should evolve. An effective leader recognizes the importance of periodically reviewing and adapting the vision and mission to reflect new realities, challenges, and opportunities. This flexibility allows the organization to remain relevant and at the forefront of its industry.

Stakeholder Engagement:

To ensure that the vision and mission are authentic and genuinely represent the essence of the organization, involving various stakeholders in their development and revision is crucial. This may include employees, customers, partners, and other stakeholders. A collaborative process can lead to more robust and widely accepted statements.

While one might think that defining vision and mission is a straightforward exercise, their creation, implementation, and maintenance require deep reflection, ongoing commitment, and a clear understanding of the broader landscape in which an organization operates. The challenges and opportunities that arise from navigating this territory are endless but also fundamental to long-term growth and success.

Measurement and Evaluation:

Every vision and mission statement should have associated measurement and evaluation mechanisms. Without these, it becomes challenging for an organization to know whether it is actually progressing toward its desired vision or fulfilling its mission. Tools such as budget frameworks, key performance

indicators (KPIs), and periodic surveys among
stakeholders can provide valuable data on how close or
far an organization is from achieving these objectives.

Communication:

Vision and mission should not be stagnant texts kept in
an office manual. They should be actively
communicated both internally and externally. Within
an organization, this ensures that all company
members are aligned and mobilized toward common
goals. Externally, it helps define the organization's
public identity and build trust with customers,
partners, and other stakeholders.

Emotional Resonance:

The most effective vision and mission statements are
those that resonate emotionally. It's not just about
what an organization does or where it wants to go but
why it matters. This emotional resonance can motivate
and inspire people, creating a sense of purpose that
goes beyond simple business objectives.

Training and Integration:

For new hires or those entering an organization,
introduction and assimilation into the company's
vision and mission are crucial. Through training and
integration programs, new team members can quickly
understand the organization's fundamental objectives

and how their individual roles contribute to achieving them.

Periodic Reflection:

Over time, circumstances change, industries evolve, and companies grow in new directions. As such, it's vital for organizations to periodically reflect on their current vision and mission. This may include strategic retreats, brainstorming sessions, and consultations with external experts.

External Factors:

External forces, such as market trends, regulatory changes, or global crises, can have a significant impact on the validity or relevance of an existing vision or mission. Organizations must be prepared to adapt and update their statements in response to such forces, while ensuring that any changes remain true to the organization's core values.

The Role of Technology:

With the advancement of digital technologies, the ways in which vision and mission statements are communicated and implemented are changing. Social media platforms, interactive websites, and corporate applications are just some of the ways organizations can now connect with a broader audience and ensure that their vision and mission are visible and accessible.

In conclusion, while vision and mission are fundamental concepts, their management and implementation are complex and multifaceted. They require ongoing attention, adaptability, and a deep understanding of both the organization's internal landscape and the external environments in which it operates.

Vision and Mission:

Vision and mission are fundamental pillars upon which an organization is built and guided. They represent, respectively, the long-term goal that an entity aims to achieve and its fundamental purpose within the ecosystem in which it operates.

Meaning and Interconnection:

Vision is an ideal representation of the future that an organization aspires to create or achieve. It serves as a beacon, guiding strategic decisions and providing a reference point for assessing progress. In contrast, the mission focuses on the present, describing the primary reason why an organization exists and how it intends to serve its stakeholders.

Resonance and Communication:

Vision and mission must be easily understood and resonate with all stakeholders, both internal and external. If well articulated and communicated, they can motivate employees, attract customers and partners, and set an organization apart from its competitors. Transparency in communication and consistency in action are essential to maintain trust and alignment with these statements.

Adaptability and Reflection:

In the ever-changing context of modern business, even the deepest and well-formulated vision and mission statements may require revisions. Organizations must be prepared to review and adapt these statements in response to internal or external changes. This process of reflection not only ensures relevance but also strengthens the organization's commitment to its purpose and objectives.

Technology and Innovation:

In the digital age, the ways in which vision and mission are shared and implemented have undergone significant changes. Technology offers new platforms and tools to communicate, monitor, and pursue these objectives, making it easier than ever for organizations to remain connected and aligned with their core values in innovative ways.

Conclusion:

Ultimately, vision and mission are not mere statements to put on a website or an office poster. They are the beating heart of an organization. They represent the deepest aspirations, ethical guidance, and preferred path. When well understood, shared, and consistently pursued, they can transform an entity from a mere organization into a movement that truly embodies the change it seeks to bring about in the world.

Feedback and Leadership:

The Importance of Ongoing Feedback for Growth and Adaptation.

Feedback is an essential component of the development process, both for organizations and individuals. In the realm of leadership, feedback becomes even more crucial because leaders are responsible not only for their personal development but also for the success and growth of the people and teams they lead.

The Role of Feedback in Leadership:

Feedback provides a window into others' perceptions of your actions and decisions. For leaders, this can reveal gaps in communication, areas for improvement in strategy or people management, and offer ideas for new directions or approaches. Without constructive feedback, a leader might operate in a vacuum, unaware of potential issues or opportunities.

Feedback for Growth:

Every leader, regardless of experience or success, has areas where they can improve. Feedback offers a clear understanding of these areas, allowing leaders to address specific weaknesses or develop new skills. This continuous growth not only benefits the leader but also enhances the effectiveness and resilience of the entire organization.

Adaptation and Change:

The business world is constantly changing, and what worked yesterday may not work tomorrow. Feedback can help leaders recognize when it's time to change direction, adapt a strategy, or revise an approach. Being receptive to feedback means being ready to adapt in response to the evolving needs of the market, customers, or employees.

Creating a Feedback Culture:

For feedback to be effective, there must be an organizational culture in which people feel free and encouraged to share their opinions and perceptions. This requires an environment in which feedback is seen as a gift, not as criticism, and where open communication is valued and promoted.

Two-Way Feedback:

While leaders must be open to receiving feedback, it's also essential that they provide regular feedback to members of their team. This type of communication can motivate, educate, and guide individuals toward achieving their goals while providing clarity and recognition for the work done.

The art of feedback in leadership goes beyond merely sharing opinions and perceptions. It's a dynamic process that, when well-managed, can serve as a catalyst for transformation at both the individual and organizational levels.

Feedback as a Mirror:

A leader who encourages feedback effectively invites others to hold a mirror up to them. This mirror reflects the often-hidden realities of their leadership style and actions. For example, a leader might think they are very open and approachable, but feedback might reveal that team members feel intimidated or excluded. This kind of feedback-guided introspection is vital for authentic growth.

The Temporal Aspect of Feedback:

Timeliness is essential when it comes to feedback. Receiving feedback on an incident or decision months after it occurred reduces its relevance and impact. Therefore, leaders should create mechanisms to receive feedback in real-time or as close to the event in question as possible.

Positive Feedback vs. Constructive Feedback:

While positive feedback reinforces desirable behaviors and actions, constructive feedback identifies areas for improvement. Both are essential for leadership. Positive feedback serves as reinforcement, motivating the leader and the team to continue on a certain trajectory. Constructive feedback, on the other hand, provides an opportunity for learning and growth.

Tools and Platforms for Feedback:

In the age of digitalization, numerous platforms and tools are available that facilitate the feedback process. From survey applications to performance management systems, these platforms can provide quantitative and qualitative feedback, offering leaders a detailed overview of perceptions.

Vulnerability in Receiving Feedback:

Receiving feedback, especially when it's not flattering, requires a certain level of vulnerability. Leaders must be ready to accept that they won't always be right and that there will be moments when their actions may not resonate well with others. This openness to vulnerability, however, is what allows genuine growth and authenticity in leadership.

The Psychology of Feedback:

From a psychological perspective, feedback has a profound impact on self-esteem and self-efficacy. Leaders who regularly receive feedback and act accordingly tend to have greater confidence in their abilities. Similarly, providing regular and relevant feedback can improve team morale and engagement.

Lastly, feedback is not just a practice but also a skill. Like all skills, it requires practice, patience, and perseverance. But the benefits, both for leaders and organizations, are immense and can lead to a more harmonious, productive, and innovative work environment.

Feedback and Organizational Culture:

Feedback is not just a tool for improving individual performance but can also shape the culture of an entire organization. An environment where feedback is encouraged, valued, and regularly given can foster a climate of openness, transparency, and mutual commitment. In such organizations, individuals are more likely to share their ideas, express concerns, and actively participate in collective growth.

Respect in the Feedback Process:

For feedback to be effectively received and considered, it must be presented respectfully. The art of giving feedback is as much about "how" as it is about "what." Critically or aggressively delivered feedback can easily be rejected or cause defensiveness. Therefore, it is crucial for leaders to learn to share feedback constructively, providing specific observations and offering solutions or suggestions for improvement.

Feedback and Diversity:

In a global and multicultural context, feedback can vary significantly in terms of style and expectations. What might be seen as direct and helpful feedback in one culture could be perceived as blunt or insensitive in another. Therefore, leaders must be culturally sensitive when giving and receiving feedback, having an awareness of diverse cultural norms and adapting accordingly.

Self-Feedback:

In addition to receiving feedback from others, it is crucial for leaders to develop the ability to self-assess. This self-feedback allows leaders to reflect on their actions, decisions, and behaviors, autonomously identifying areas of strength and areas for improvement. Tools like reflection journals or meditation can assist in this introspective process.

Feedback as an Engagement Tool:

When team members feel that their opinions are heard and valued, they tend to feel more appreciated and engaged in their work. Feedback can thus serve as a powerful engagement tool, reinforcing a sense of belonging and identification with the organization.

Avoiding Feedback Overload:

While regular feedback is beneficial, there is also a risk of feedback overload, where too many comments and suggestions can become overwhelming and counterproductive. Leaders must find a balance, ensuring that the feedback provided is relevant, timely, and manageable.

Feedback is one of the most vital components in the leadership landscape. Its presence, when effectively managed, can not only shape a leader's growth path but can also steer an entire organization's trajectory toward success and innovation.

The Importance of Feedback in the Professional World:

In a rapidly changing and ever-evolving work environment, feedback provides a compass. It offers a clear indication of what is working and what isn't, allowing leaders and teams to make timely adjustments. Without effective feedback, organizations risk navigating blindly, missing opportunities, and facing inefficiencies.

Feedback as a Growth Tool:

From an individual perspective, feedback is a vehicle for personal and professional growth. It enables individuals to understand their strengths and areas where improvement is needed. For leaders, in particular, receiving feedback from subordinates, peers, and superiors can provide a comprehensive view of their skills and leadership style.

Creating a Positive Feedback Environment:

However, for feedback to be effective, it is essential to create an environment where it is given and received constructively. This requires an organizational culture where feedback is not seen as criticism but as an opportunity. It also necessitates training leaders and employees on how to give and receive feedback that is specific, clear, and action-oriented.

Feedback and Organizational Change:

At a macro level, feedback can serve as a catalyst for organizational change. It can identify areas where business processes are inefficient or where corporate culture could be improved. In this sense, feedback benefits not only individuals but the entire organization.

Challenges of Feedback:

Naturally, there are challenges associated with feedback. It can be difficult for some to receive, especially when it's critical. Similarly, giving feedback, especially negative or constructive feedback, can be a challenge in itself. However, with the right training and culture, these challenges can be overcome.

In conclusion, feedback is fundamental in modern leadership. It allows leaders to better understand themselves, the people they lead, and the organization they operate in. When integrated correctly, feedback can guide personal growth, enhance team productivity, and steer the entire trajectory of an organization toward success and excellence. Therefore, investing in creating a feedback

culture and training on how to give and receive feedback is essential for any leader or organization aspiring to achieve excellence.

20. Future Trends: Where Is Leadership Heading? Exploring Future Perspectives.

In the context of a constantly evolving world and an increasingly dynamic business environment, leadership is undergoing several significant transformations. By examining current trends and attempting to foresee future directions, we can identify some key elements that are likely to have a lasting impact on the leadership landscape in the coming years.

1. **Distributed Leadership:**

In the past, leadership was often centralized and hierarchical. However, with the increasing complexity of organizations and the need for rapid and adaptive decision-making, we see a trend toward distributed leadership. This means that more people within an organization will have leadership roles, enabling greater agility and a faster response to emerging challenges.

2. Holistic Leadership:

There is a growing awareness of the importance of overall well-being, both physically and mentally. Future leaders will be those who recognize the importance of looking at the whole person, supporting not only professional goals but also the personal well-being of their employees.

3. Values-Based Leadership:

While profit remains a priority for many businesses, there is a growing emphasis on creating value in terms of social and environmental impact. Future leaders will be those who can successfully balance profit and purpose, guiding their organizations toward sustainable and ethical solutions.

4. Leadership and Artificial Intelligence:

With the rapid evolution of technology and the adoption of artificial intelligence in many sectors, leaders will need to understand how to effectively integrate these technologies into their strategies while ensuring that humanity remains at the core of decision-making.

5. Inclusive Leadership:

Diversity and inclusion are becoming increasingly central. Future leaders will be those who truly embrace diversity, not just as a "to-do" but as a key component of success. This includes promoting an inclusive culture where every voice is heard and valued.

6. **Continuous Growth-Based Leadership:**

Continuous learning will become even more crucial. With ongoing technological and market developments, leaders must be in a constant state of learning and adaptation, remaining open to new ideas and changes.

7. **Global Leadership:**

With the rise of globalization and increased interconnection between markets and cultures, the ability to operate and lead on a global scale will become even more essential. This will require a deep understanding of diverse cultures and market dynamics.

In summary, future leadership will be less rigid, more fluid, and will require a combination of technical, emotional, and interpersonal skills. The ability to adapt quickly to changes while maintaining a strong sense of direction and purpose will be essential. Leaders will also need to balance immediate needs with a long-term vision, guiding their organizations toward a sustainable and prosperous future.

The Evolution of Leadership Continues: Exploring Future Trends:

Adoption of Emerging Technologies:

While artificial intelligence represents a significant breakthrough, other technologies like virtual reality, augmented reality, and blockchain are beginning to shape how businesses operate. Future leaders will need to understand how these technologies can be integrated into daily operations, forming specialized teams, and ensuring that these technological solutions are used ethically and responsibly.

Leadership Through Crises and Uncertainty:

With the acceleration of climate change, global political tensions, and challenges like pandemics or natural disasters, leaders must be prepared to navigate moments of profound uncertainty. This will require flexibility, predictability, and the ability to make tough decisions even when not all information is available.

Focus on Education and Continuous Training:

The concept of "lifelong learning" is gaining ground. With the rapid evolution of professions and required skills, leaders will need to emphasize the importance of continuous training, creating opportunities for employees to update and enhance their skills.

Health and Well-being:

In addition to mental health, there will be a growing focus on physical well-being. Companies may adopt more holistic approaches, incorporating practices like mindfulness, meditation, and physical exercise into the daily routine to ensure that employees are at their best both mentally and physically.

Sustainability and Environmental Responsibility:

Sustainability awareness is growing, not only in terms of green business practices. Leaders will be called upon to think about how their decisions impact the environment in the long term and seek innovative solutions to reduce their companies' ecological footprint.

Active Listening and Engagement:

In the digital world, with information overload, active listening becomes crucial. Leaders will need to refine their listening skills, ensuring that every team member feels heard and valued. This will also help create a more inclusive work environment.

Building Partnerships and Collaborations:

The complexity of modern problems often requires collaborative solutions. Leaders will need to actively seek partnerships and collaborations, both within and outside their industries, to create innovative solutions to common challenges.

Balancing Technology and Humanity:

Even with the widespread adoption of technology, the human element will remain fundamental. Leaders will need to strike a balance, ensuring that technology is used to enhance the human experience rather than replace it.

These are just some of the many aspects shaping the future direction of leadership. While each trend brings a set of opportunities, it also presents challenges that leaders must proactively address.

In conclusion, future leadership will be a dynamic synthesis of old fundamental principles and new skills acquired in response to the evolving global context. The unprecedented speed of technological, social, and economic change demands leaders who are grounded in traditions of integrity, vision, and compassion, while equipped with the flexibility to adapt to new challenges.

Key Aspects of Future Leadership:

1. **Technology and Humanity:**

Future leaders will have the crucial task of bridging the gap between technological innovation and the essence of humanity. Striking a balance between automation and human capabilities, leveraging technology to improve people's lives rather than replacing them, will be paramount.

2. **Adaptability and Resilience:**

Emerging challenges, from environmental crises to geopolitical tensions, will require leaders capable of quickly adapting to new scenarios and guiding their organizations through turbulent times with firmness and vision.

3. **Continuous Education:**

Learning will no longer be seen as a transitional phase of life but as an ongoing commitment. Leaders must promote a culture of learning within their organizations, encouraging continuous training and professional development.

4. **Sustainability and Long-Term Vision:**

Immediate success will no longer be the sole criterion for success. Leaders will be evaluated based on their ability to think and act in the long term, ensuring that their decisions are sustainable and beneficial not only for their organization but also for society and the environment at large.

5. **Listening and Inclusivity:**

Diversity and inclusion will be at the heart of future leadership. Leaders must ensure that all voices are heard and decisions are made considering a variety of perspectives. This will contribute to creating stronger, more resilient, and innovative organizations.

6. **Collaboration Beyond Borders:**

In an increasingly interconnected world, the ability to collaborate beyond geographical, cultural, and sectoral boundaries will be essential. Co-creation, joint innovation, and partnerships will be essential tools in leaders' toolkits.

In summary, future leadership will require a unique combination of skills, both old and new. Leaders must be anchored in core values while being ready to embrace change, seize new opportunities, and confront challenges with an open and innovative mindset. The path to future leadership will be as exciting as it is challenging, but with the right preparation and mindset, leaders will be able to navigate this new landscape successfully and lead their organizations toward a prosperous and sustainable future.

Book Summary: Leadership in the 21st Century

Leadership is both an art and a science, and as such, it is subject to changes and developments. Throughout this book, we have explored the wide range of aspects that define and influence leadership in today's dynamic context.

1. **Culture and Leadership:** We discussed how various cultures influence leadership expectations and styles, emphasizing the importance of adaptability and intercultural awareness.

2. **Female Leadership:** We analyzed the significance and uniqueness of female leadership, highlighting its specific contributions in the modern world.

3. **Leadership Challenges:** This point touched on conflict management, active listening, empathy, and resilience, all essential for effective leadership.

4. **Leadership and Ethics:** We discussed the crucial moral responsibility of leaders and the indispensable importance of integrity.

5. **Techniques and Tools:** Here, we offered practical tips to refine and develop leadership skills.

6. **Leadership and Innovation:** We explored how leaders can promote and support innovation within their organizations.

7. **Leadership Training:** We emphasized the importance of continuous training for leaders' growth.

8. **Case Studies:** They provided tangible examples of leadership in action, illustrating both successes and failures.

9. **Digital Leadership:** Here, we discussed the importance of navigating the digital revolution with competence and vision.

10. **Leadership and Mental Health:** We addressed stress management, burnout, and the importance of self-care.

11. **Teams and Leadership:** We talked about creating, leading, and maintaining high-performance teams.

12. **Vision and Mission:** We emphasized the importance of having a clear vision and mission.

13. **Feedback and Leadership:** We discussed the importance of continuous feedback for growth and adaptation.

14. **Future Trends:** This section offered a glimpse into the future prospects of leadership.

Additional Resources: For those who wish to delve further into these topics, here are some online resources:

- **Harvard Business Review (HBR):** An excellent resource for articles and case studies on leadership.

    - Website: hbr.org

- **Leadership Now:** Provides insights and resources on various aspects of leadership.

    - Website: leadershipnow.com

- **Center for Creative Leadership (CCL):** A resource dedicated to leadership training and development.

    - Website: ccl.org

- **Gallup's StrengthsFinder:** A tool that helps leaders identify and cultivate their strengths.

    - Website: gallupstrengthscenter.com

In conclusion, leadership is a journey, not a destination. As challenges and circumstances change, the essence of leadership remains constant: influencing and inspiring others toward a common goal. Keep educating yourself, testing your abilities, and seeking growth opportunities. Your leadership journey is unique, and we hope this book has provided you with insights and tools to navigate it successfully.